WHAT

RIGHT

WITH

KANSAS

EVERYDAY CITIZENS TRANSFORMING THEIR STATE

ED O'MALLEY
FOREWORD BY STEVE COEN

THIS BOOK IS DEDICATED TO THE
KANSAS LEADERSHIP CENTER FAMILY.

KLC Press
Kansas Leadership Center
325 East Douglas, Wichita, KS, USA, 67202
Visit our website at www.kansasleadershipcenter.org.
This edition published in 2018.
Library of Congress Control Number: 2017952646
ISBN: 978-0-692-93787-7

Cover and layout designed by Clare McClaren, Novella Brandhouse
Illustrations by Stamp Yo Face
Photos: Stocksy.com

Printed in the United States of America

 KLC PRESS

www.WhatsRightWithKansas.com

Table of Contents

FOREWORD
BY STEVE COEN

"UNLESS someone like you cares a whole awful lot, nothing is going to get better. It's not."

"THE LORAX," DR. SEUSS

Many times the lessons we learn as children can help guide us through complicated problems in life, if we look for the simple messages. Like the Lorax, we at the Kansas Health Foundation (KHF) found that the key to building leadership capacity in Kansas is getting people in communities to care enough about something to step up and make change happen. Lots of people can dream up the solutions or ideas, but it takes someone who "cares a whole awful lot" to lead.

Between 1992 and 2005, KHF coordinated various initiatives on leadership, including the Leadership Institute, the KHF Leadership Conference, the Kansas Community Leadership Initiative, 21st Century Leadership and the KHF Fellows program. These all helped to create greater awareness of health policy issues, specific community needs and tools for how to bring people together to find a shared perspective. Through these efforts we learned that offering training to people to build leadership infrastructure in their communities was key to tackling complex health and wellness issues.

We made the bold step to emphasize the strong relationship between leadership and stronger, healthier Kansas communities through a 10-year, $30 million grant to start the Kansas Leadership Center (KLC). The KLC is able to bring together Kansans from neighborhoods, businesses, nonprofit organizations, churches and government entities because it cares a whole awful lot about making things better. But probably as important as the leadership training these individuals receive, they make connections with other Kansans, giving them exponential power to do good!

So here we are, 25 years after KHF started engaging Kansans to care enough to lead, and 10 years since the KLC first encouraged participants to think about adaptive challenges and leadership as an activity. This deliberate focus on building leadership capacity has evolved into a heightened level of civic engagement. Not only do these leaders help address health problems where they live, they work to engage more Kansans to create solutions to a myriad of community challenges. Having active residents means stronger civic health, which results in a better quality of life in the community. And we need stronger communities for healthier people.

It would be easy to be overwhelmed by the many daunting challenges in our state. But fortunately, Kansans are leading efforts every day to make this a better place to work, live and play. It simply starts with someone caring a whole awful lot.

I hope you enjoy these stories of everyday Kansans who are creating a positive change within their communities and that it inspires you to do the same.

STEVE COEN
President & CEO, Kansas Health Foundation

INTRODUCTION

"If it's going to happen, it'll happen first in Kansas."

ED O'MALLEY
President & CEO,
Kansas Leadership Center

William Allen White, the great Kansan, newspaper publisher and friend to Teddy Roosevelt, offered that quote above. The Civil War was sparked in Kansas. Women had some voting rights in Kansas long before any other state. Social turmoil from the populist revolt in the 1890s to the Summer of Mercy abortion protests of the 1980s found their home first in Kansas.

"What's the Matter with Kansas?" was the title of William Allen White's famous editorial from the Emporia Gazette in 1896. The editorial railed against the populist revolt in Kansas but more importantly put White, the Emporia, Kansas newspaper publisher, in the national consciousness. He became the most famous small-town newspaper man of his age. Kansas became a symbol of the nation.

Generations later Thomas Frank's 2004 book "What's the Matter with Kansas?" used Kansas as a metaphor for much of what Frank thought was wrong with politics in America.

This book is not a rebuke of White's column or Frank's book, but it is a celebration of something that is indeed very right with Kansas: a type of leadership that is taking hold across the state and leading to more progress on what people care most about.

And this type of leadership, which will be described throughout this book, is flourishing across our state and sparking similar efforts outside Kansas. We are becoming yet another "Kansas first." That's a good thing. Our nation and world need a surge of real leadership, a tonic to our polarized times. Look to Kansas to understand what's to come. It's been true in our past and is true again.

What's the matter with Kansas? I'm an optimist and that question bores me.

We've had our share of dysfunction born out of policy and leadership at the statehouse. Our tax and budget battles have been regular fodder for New York Times and Wall Street Journal editorial boards. Our state economy lags neighboring states. The divide between urban and rural Kansas deepens. What's the matter with Kansas? Our politics is a mismatch for our times.

Continued globalization and rapid advancement in technology require collaboration and engagement to discover the adaptations necessary to thrive. What we've received from our state-level politics is bickering, isolation, estrangement, middle-school-like bullying and silliness. Enough has been written about the dysfunction of Kansas statehouse politics. This book focuses on the leadership, at a massive scale, bubbling up from beneath, the leadership that is changing organizations and communities and solving problems.

What's right with Kansas? Thousands of Kansans exercising the type of leadership described in this book, for the greater good of their organizations and the common good of our communities.

This book describes the principles of leadership these Kansans have embraced and will help you do the same.

I want these principles firmly embedded in Kansas. That work has begun and this book tells that story.

MAYBE THE BATTER DOESN'T EVEN SEE THE PITCH.

Or maybe he sees it but keeps the bat on his shoulder. Maybe he swings, knowing intellectually the odds aren't in his favor but believing emotionally he will succeed. And maybe he will see the ball just right, connect and send the ball into the gap, advancing a runner and helping his team.

In baseball, if you hit the ball on average just three out of 10 times you'll be one of the best. You will be enshrined in the Baseball Hall of Fame in Cooperstown, New York. Your .300 batting average will be the envy of players and kids everywhere. But you would have failed seven out of 10 times at the plate. Seventy percent of the time you would have struck out, grounded out or popped out.

The understanding that even the best fail more than they succeed creates a humbleness rarely seen among many professionals.

What if that same understanding was embedded in our collective thinking about leadership? I can assure you it should be after 10 years of working with thousands of Kansans and others trying hard to exercise leadership.

This book is designed to help you think about your own leadership, to provoke you to consider a set of leadership principles that will help you make more of a difference wherever you choose to lead.

We each have a "leadership average," but when we walk into a room, that average isn't flashed on a jumbo scoreboard. Wouldn't it be fascinating if it was?

The difference between a Hall of Famer and someone who can't even make the roster is just one hit in 10.

Hit .300 and you are a star. Hit .200 and you'll fall below the Mendoza Line, in baseball parlance, and you probably won't even make it in the minors. The only difference is one hit out of every 10 chances.

What if the difference between the best leaders and the mediocre were that slim as well? I think it is. Would we be more forgiving of those we expect to lead? Would we be thrilled when they do it well, when they connect and help mobilize a group, company, community, state or nation? But would we also understand that most of their efforts, probably seven out of 10, wouldn't work?

People who attempt to exercise leadership often get defensive when things don't work out. A politician spins the facts. A CEO over-explains the strategy. A community official does whatever possible to make it look like whatever had been done was a success. What if an official could just say, "I didn't see that one all too well. I'll work on a few things and be back at it tomorrow." I think their constituencies would accept that, because they would know leadership isn't something that someone can do all the time. Just like it's not possible to hit .800 or .900 in baseball.

Personally, I think I fail at exercising leadership more than I succeed. Knowing that makes it easier to hear the criticism, constructive or otherwise, from others. But criticism need not inspire a defensive stance, because there is nothing to defend. Of course I'm not perfect. Of course I don't always lead well. Of course, of course, of course. Now help me get better.

The difference between hovering at the Mendoza Line or achieving Hall of Fame credentials is the steady application of practice, discernment, practice and more discernment, all eventually and optimistically leading to our being just a bit better. In baseball and in leadership.

THE KANSAS LEADERSHIP CENTER EXISTS TO
INCREASE THE "LEADERSHIP AVERAGE" OF KANSANS.

My last book, "Your Leadership Edge: Lead Anytime, Anywhere" (co-authored with Amanda Cebula), described the four competencies of leadership taught at the KLC: Diagnose Situation, Manage Self, Intervene Skillfully and Energize Others. Those competencies describe the behaviors of leadership. This book focuses on the principles that underpin those behaviors.

For example, it's because "leadership is risky" (the fifth principle described in this book) that it's necessary to "speak to loss" (part of Energize Others) and "act experimentally" (part of Intervene Skillfully).

And it's because "your purpose must be clear" (the fourth principle described in this book) that it's necessary to "choose among competing values" (part of Manage Self). A brief note describing the four competencies appears after this introduction.

Working on a large scale — directly with a couple of thousand people each year and indirectly with thousands and thousands more — we are trying to imbed the leadership principles described in this book throughout our state. We help countless others imbed these leadership principles in their organizations, communities or companies. On behalf of everyone at the KLC, we hope this book inspires you to do the same for your organization. You can be a part of this story if you are a Kansan. You too can live out these principles in your civic engagement, imbed them in your organization or community. Do your part to help bring forth a Kansas for tomorrow.

If you are not a Kansan, use the Kansas metaphor to inspire your own use of these leadership principles.

SO, IF WE WANT TO UP OUR LEADERSHIP AVERAGE,
TO BECOME A BIT MORE SUCCESSFUL AT MOBILIZING
OTHERS, WE NEED A GOOD UNDERSTANDING OF WHAT
LEADERSHIP ACTUALLY IS.

Let's get a few definitions out of the way, for the purpose of this book.

Leadership is mobilizing others to make progress on daunting challenges.

Principles are fundamental truths that serve as the foundation for beliefs or for a chain of reasoning.

What are your leadership principles? What are the principles that underpin your efforts to mobilize others to make progress on daunting challenges? When you have a tough challenge before you, what principles guide your actions? What are the leadership principles of your organization or company? Consciously or subconsciously, they exist.

If I asked someone who knows you, what would they say your leadership principles are?

Here are some examples.

XYZ Inc. has 2,000 employees. Upper management hand-selects 12 individuals annually for its corporate leadership program. The program consists of three retreats over the course of the year led by the CEO. What are the leadership principles? The following might come to mind:

> *Leadership is for the select few.*
>
> *Leadership can be best identified by those with lots of power and authority.*
>
> *Leadership is best taught by the CEO.*

A state agency has been struggling the past few years. Crisis after crisis hits the agency, most of which are self-inflicted. The public is losing confidence. Legislators are launching audits and there is a revolving door in the senior roles. There is no effort to build leadership capacity among the staff. As struggles worsen, management holds more closed-door meetings of the senior team. What are the leadership principles? The following might come to mind:

> *Transparency is dangerous.*
>
> *Leadership can't be developed.*
>
> *Management is solely responsible for leadership.*

An elected official has served a few terms. She is constantly busy, running from event to event. Since taking office she has spent less time with her family, often missing important events of her school-aged children. She holds town hall meetings each month where she answers questions from constituents, with her speaking probably 90 percent of the meeting. Each year she proposes and is often successful in passing a minor, niche piece of legislation (which she usually talks a lot about at her town hall meetings). What are the leadership principles? The following come to mind:

> *Being exhausted is part of leadership.*
>
> *Leadership is about answering questions.*
>
> *Leadership is about the small stuff.*

What leadership principles would come to mind if someone observed your organization or you?

What leadership principles are needed for progress on what you and your people care most about?

This book suggests five leadership principles that, if they are embodied by your organization or initiative, lead to progress on the leadership challenges you and others care most about. These challenges tend to be adaptive in nature, meaning there is no quick fix (despite our desire to find one!) and that transformation will be required if progress is to be made.

Our friends Marty Linsky and Ron Heifetz introduced us to the framing of adaptive challenges versus technical problems. The latter are solved with experts or authority alone. The former are solved with a type of leadership, coming from enough people within the organization or community, that helps mobilize a system to change.

I've been blessed to have Marty as a dear friend and mentor. He has traveled the world working with thousands of committed individuals working to make progress on their adaptive challenges.

Curious about what adaptive challenges are facing you? *When you think about the future of your organization/company/community, what concerns you the most? When you think about the future of your organization/company/community, what is your greatest aspiration?*

The answers will most likely be adaptive challenges, issues or situations that no one knows exactly how to solve. Adaptive challenges are about letting go of parts of our current reality and embracing new attitudes and behaviors necessary to survive and thrive.

WHERE DID THESE PRINCIPLES COME FROM?

Ten years of deep listening, engagement and learning from thousands of good-hearted individuals and groups, trying to make the world around them — their communities and companies — better, more productive and more impactful.

These are the principles that form the foundation of the Kansas Leadership Center and the structure for this book.

> *Leadership is an activity, not a position.*
> *Anyone can lead, anytime, anywhere.*
> *It starts with you and must engage others.*
> *Your purpose must be clear.*
> *It's risky.*

Leadership is an activity, not a position. No one has ever mobilized others to make progress on daunting challenges simply by holding a position.

Anyone can lead, anytime, anywhere. Rosa Parks taught us this, but other examples exist in history and folklore, in our practice and experience.

Leadership starts with you and must engage others. It's not a solitary activity. It is about mobilizing others, so it's never a solo thing.

Your purpose must be clear. Absent a clear purpose, you'll get nowhere. (Pro-tip: Most of us never have a clear purpose.)

Leadership is risky. Which is why we rarely see it or do it.

I hope this book inspires you to exercise leadership more frequently, to take risks for things you care about. Hold these principles close as you do, and my experience and the experience of my colleagues at the Kansas Leadership Center suggest you'll do fine.

This book gives a sampling of the stories of leadership permeating across Kansas. Many of these stories were first reported in our award-winning magazine, The Journal, which has become a powerful force in civic life in our state. Working directly with around 2,000 individuals each year in extensive experiences and influencing many more through our publications and speaking engagements, all the stories of leadership stemming from this work can't be tracked let alone told. There are thousands of flowers — sunflowers — blooming in Kansas. You'll read about some of them here.

Onward!

LEARN MORE ABOUT THE ORIGINS OF THESE IDEAS IN "FOR THE COMMON GOOD: REDEFINING CIVIC LEADERSHIP," OUR FIRST BOOK. VISIT WWW.KLCJOURNAL.COM TO READ MORE STORIES OF LEADERSHIP TRANSFORMING OUR STATE.

The Leadership Competencies

The next page is a snapshot of the four competencies taught at the KLC. The competencies are simple, yet provocative. They are easy to understand, yet very rare to see in practice. Dive into "Your Leadership Edge: Lead Anytime, Anywhere" or attend a KLC program to learn more.

The four competencies exist because of the principles described in this book. If you believe, like we do, that the five principles described here are truths – that leadership is risky, that your purpose must be clear, that leadership involves other people, that anyone can lead and that leadership is an activity – then the competencies on the next page are the way in which you lead.

The principles in this book are the foundation for all the behaviors and ideas taught at the KLC. Together, the KLC principles and competencies create a framework that is transforming leadership across Kansas.

Diagnose Situation

- *Explore tough interpretations*
- *Distinguish technical and adaptive work*
- *Understand the process challenges*
- *Test multiple interpretations and points of view*
- *Take the temperature*
- *Identify who needs to do the work*

Manage Self

- *Know your strengths, vulnerabilities and triggers*
- *Know the story others tell about you*
- *Choose among competing values*
- *Get used to uncertainty and conflict*
- *Experiment beyond your comfort zone*
- *Take care of yourself*

Energize Others

- *Engage unusual voices*
- *Work across factions*
- *Start where they are*
- *Speak to loss*
- *Inspire a collective purpose*
- *Create a trustworthy process*

Intervene Skillfully

- *Make conscious choices*
- *Raise the heat*
- *Give the work back*
- *Hold to purpose*
- *Speak from the heart*
- *Act experimentally*

KANSAS LEADERSHIP CENTER

Leadership Principle № 1

IT WAS MAY 1, 2007, AND I WAS SPEAKING TO A GROUP IN KANSAS ABOUT LEADERSHIP – A TOPIC I WOULD DEDICATE THE NEXT DECADE TO UNDERSTANDING BUT AT THAT POINT HAD ONLY BEEN THINKING CRITICALLY ABOUT FOR A FEW MONTHS.

As the CEO of a growing organization and a former elected official, I give a lot of speeches – thousands in the past 20 years. But that 2007 speech stands out to me. It was not a particularly good speech. I stumbled through, trying to describe an idea that wasn't quite ripe in my mind.

I remember it to this day for one reason: That was the first time I talked about leadership as an activity, not a position.

Leadership is an *activity,* not a *position.*

I was oblivious to the distinction before that day.

And in my oblivion, if someone had suggested to me that leadership was an activity, not a position, I surely would have nodded my head and replied with something such as, "Yes, it's about what you do and how you do it that counts!" But I would have totally missed the point.

It wasn't until that day that I began to separate the idea of leadership from the idea of authority. Prior to that, while I would have agreed that leadership is all about behaviors and actions and activities, I would have assumed, subconsciously, that leadership is a set of actions for those in *certain positions*. You see, I would have still been confusing leadership with authority.

I was 32 years old on May 1, 2007. It had taken me 32 years to figure out what someday will be obvious in Kansas, that leadership is an activity, not a position. Thirty-two years!

Countless times over those 32 years, I had failed to exercise leadership simply because I wasn't in a key role or position.

I'm sure there were moments on the playground, when a bully was being a bully, that someone (myself included) could have exercised the leadership to intervene. But it's the teacher's job to solve that problem, right?

I'm sure there were times in my family life when leadership from me would have helped my mom and dad. Maybe my leadership could have calmed tensions in the family, helped end an argument or raised a tough issue that a sibling or cousin needed to wrestle with. But all that stuff was supposed to be Mom or Dad's job, right?

In college, I'm sure there were times when a professor was struggling, not on his game, and the class wasn't learning a thing, just going through the motions. I'm sure there were things I could have done to energize the class, fuel the learning. Heck, I could have just stated that it appeared no one was learning!

That would have raised the heat and perhaps propelled us to more productive engagement. But all that was the professor's job, right?

In my early career, I'm sure there were times when I saw a problem with the company strategy. But that's the CEO's job, right?

Just think about all the times we fail to exercise leadership because we are so used to thinking that leadership and authority go hand in hand.

I didn't know it at the time, but in that May Day speech in 2007 I was beginning to map out what our Kansas Leadership Center team would later list as our first principle of leadership: *Leadership is an activity, not a position.*

We weren't the originators of the idea, but everything else at KLC — the curriculum, our programs, the challenges we've met and the support we've provided — flows from that foundation. An unorganized, rambling speech set in motion a leadership framework designed to help people dramatically increase their ability to exercise leadership, no matter their position.

JONATHAN LONG IS LIVING THIS PRINCIPLE. HE GREW UP IN CHATTANOOGA, TENNESSEE, ONLY ABOUT 100 MILES FROM ATLANTA, WHERE AFRICAN-AMERICAN HIGHER EDUCATION AND BUSINESS SUCCESS HAD ESTABLISHED A BLACK MECCA OF SORTS FOR ACHIEVEMENT.

But in his transplanted home of Wichita, the lack of engagement among his peers and, worse, the sense among them that engagement was impossible given historical barriers, left him puzzled about how best to move forward.

"A lot of that felt systemic," he said of his peers' reluctance to venture outside the comfort of outsider status. "And a lot of that was just not feeling like they wanted to be a part."

"A lot of that disengagement comes from people feeling as though they couldn't exercise leadership without having a position."

JONATHAN LONG
Founder, Wichita Urban Professionals

The outsider/insider dynamic is a powerful mindset that locks so many into thinking leadership is a position. They look at those in power in a company, organization or community, don't see anyone like them, and conclude there is nothing they can do. They can't lead because they don't have the power.

Jonathan's KLC experience helped him think differently.

That dearth of African-American involvement prompted him to launch Wichita Urban Professionals, an organization that promotes fellowship and networking for the city's millennial professionals.

"A lot of that disengagement comes from people feeling as though they couldn't exercise leadership without having a position," Jonathan said. "They felt like, 'I can't sit at the table because I don't have a nameplate with a position for me at the table.' Using the KLC principle that leadership is an activity, not a position, helped me push the need for something like this kind of organization."

Learning the KLC principles also filled some strategic gaps for Jonathan. "Where it really made a difference with me, it helped provide me with some framework and better understanding of things that I'd innately understood already," Jonathan said. "This really helped me. I finally had the words for what I already kind of understood. I could tell people, 'It's not just me saying this. Here's an organization (the KLC) saying the same thing. Here's a curriculum. Here's a way forward.'

"That helped get a lot of people's buy-in."

But even with this new information and language, it still wasn't easy.

He had to deal with a tentativeness on the part of prospective members. A kind of passivity, something the experience of exclusion had planted in their spirits. It remains a hurdle today.

"It takes being willing to try something different," he said. "It takes imagining yourself being successful, and that can be hard for some people because they don't even know where success starts. It takes that fundamental belief that I can really make a change, and I can be the difference.

"You have to step out on faith. You definitely have to step out on faith. You have to have the belief that this works."

Jonathan is certain that it does.

"It really does reorient your thinking," he said. "That's one of the things I love about the KLC. The KLC doesn't tell you that it's going to be easy. The KLC tells you it's going to be work. But they tell you that there's value in the work if you do it, and that is something we've seen firsthand. We have seen members of our organization become open to opportunities because they chose to act, as opposed to sitting back and saying, 'The opportunities don't exist.'"

90% OF KANSAS LEADERSHIP CENTER ALUMNI REPORT "THE KLC MATERIAL WAS IMMEDIATELY RELEVANT TO MY LIFE."

He's seen progress on one of the most intractable issues American society has faced: convincing African-Americans that engaging civically can mean engagement in a trustworthy process in which there's a real opportunity to have a stake in outcomes.

"It really helps to deal with that perception. 'Because I don't fit a certain bill, I don't look a certain way, I don't have an opportunity that someone else has,'" he said. "The doctrine of the KLC teaches you a different mindset. It teaches you more of a go-out-and-get-it mindset as opposed to letting it come to you. It teaches you that you create your own opportunities when you choose to work through these principles."

There's nobility in the struggle, he said.

"We want this to be unfamiliar and maybe uncomfortable, because our journey will be unfamiliar and uncomfortable," Jonathan said.

The way the KLC opened its facility to the effort gave his organization instant credibility and helped potential members believe they could achieve what they had been dreaming of.

"When you have a facility like that, it makes people take note," he said. "People say, 'Well, you know what, if we can come here, then maybe there is a change. Maybe I can. I can be here too.'"

BY LIVING OUT THE KLC'S PRINCIPLES, JONATHAN AND URBAN PROFESSIONALS HAVE:

Created professional opportunities.	Changed the way people think about upward professional mobility in Wichita for African-Americans.	Brought new stakeholders to the table.

WHAT'S NEXT FOR JONATHAN LONG AND URBAN PROFESSIONALS?

Continue to build on their successes and membership.

*Encourage others to engage in KLC programming
so this experience multiplies.*

IF LEADERSHIP IS AN ACTIVITY, WHAT IS THE ACTIVITY?
JONATHAN DEVELOPED HIS AND OTHERS' ABILITIES AND THE
COURAGE TO ENGAGE EVEN WITHOUT A FORMAL POSITION,
BUT WHAT EXACTLY DID THEY DO? WHAT DOES THE ACTIVITY
OF LEADERSHIP LOOK LIKE?

The activity of leadership is almost always related to creating a strong, healthy process for engagement and problem solving.

Urban Professionals is thriving, but it never would have gotten to its current state without Jonathan and fellow members engaging others and being inclusive of different perspectives.

Leadership is an activity. And it's an experimental one. Jonathan had to keep trying things. He didn't know exactly what would work to engage the African-American community. There was no expert who could tell him exactly what to do. He wasn't a "leader" because he had the idea for Urban Professionals. He "exercised leadership," sometimes successfully and sometimes not, over and over again, creating a process of engagement among many.

There is usually a direct relationship between the process used to get results and the lasting effect of those results.

TWO NATIONAL EXAMPLES:

The Affordable Care Act (aka Obamacare) became law in a bitterly divisive political battle. It's no wonder almost everything about it continues to be a bitterly divisive political battle.

The No Child Left Behind Act became law with a substantial bipartisan majority. Originally celebrated, the law has been seen as lacking ever since. But both political parties and two presidential administrations adjusted it and did so more or less with the same bipartisan spirit of the original law.

AND A BASEBALL EXAMPLE:

My beloved Kansas City Royals, under the guidance of general manager Dayton Moore, used a slow, methodical, healthy process to develop the team into a powerful contender, playing in the World Series in 2014 and winning it in 2015. Other teams might try to rush the process, only to realize that approach rarely works.

The KLC has learned that when organizations, communities and individuals get better at the process of leadership — at creating healthy, engaging processes — they create stronger, more sustainable outcomes over the long haul. And remember, progress on deep, daunting adaptive challenges almost always requires long-haul thinking.

Jonathan and the other founders of Urban Professionals set the effort up for the long haul.

Similarly, healthier processes for engagement are popping up everywhere across Kansas. Better engagement will lead to better civic initiatives. Better action by local governments. Better coordination between the public and private sectors.

SETH ETTER KNOWS THAT LEADERSHIP IS ABOUT PROCESS, THAT IT'S AN ACTIVITY. HE'S LEARNED THAT THE HARD WAY.

Seth remembers the buzz surrounding the first get-together of Open Wichita, a group that aims to foster civic involvement through technology and education.

"I think it's important for people to know you can make a difference in your community from a civic perspective. You don't have to be an elected official. You don't have to be involved in politics to make a difference. Since I am a technologist, that is the community I'm going to be involved in."

SETH ETTER | *Founder, Open Wichita*

"Civic hacking," "open data" and other concepts popular with technology-minded millennials around the country had finally found a home in Kansas.

"I think one thing I did right was generate excitement," said Seth, the group's founder. "We had a lot of people there, and a lot of projects got talked about."

But as Seth has learned in the two years since, excitement and engagement are two different things. Not that Open Wichita has been a failure — far from it, according to most people familiar with the group. But Seth said that's because he and other organizers adjusted to the reality of leadership.

"I think the problem we faced early on was none of us had experience organizing volunteers," he said.

That observation sums up a key distinction between leadership in organizational versus civic life. When it comes to adaptive challenges, no one in civic life is fully in charge. No position harnesses enough power to force the system to adapt. Even governors and mayors, when working on adaptive challenges, must work with a majority of their legislative chambers. Sure, they can act unilaterally in times of crisis, but those are often technical problems that just need someone with enough power to step in, allocate resources and make decisions. On the adaptive work — reforming schools, reviving an economy or enhancing engagement through technology, as Seth is attempting — success is often directly related to your ability to mobilize others you can't force to be mobilized.

About 30 people showed up for the inaugural meeting of Open Wichita. They talked about civic hacking, defined as sharing information and technology for the common good, and brainstormed possible projects for 10 hours — surely a sign of enthusiasm. Something was right about the process.

Seth figured there would be no shortage of folks stepping forward to do the actual work required to make projects, such as a push for greater voter participation, a reality. But that wasn't the case. "I waited around for a long time (and) put opportunities out there and hoped people would come and take them," he said.

And so Seth defaulted to what he calls a common leadership mistake: doing the work himself.

"My biggest struggle in the beginning was I felt responsible for everything in the group," Seth said. "Any work that wasn't getting done, I would do it myself. I wasn't engaging others as much as I needed to."

He was active, but he wasn't leading. Leadership is mobilizing others to make progress on daunting work. He was mostly mobilizing himself. Can't we all relate?

A mid-level worker needs help from others but has no authority over them. She takes the work on herself, stays busy, stresses over a lack of real progress and fails to adopt a new strategy.

82% OF ALUMNI AGREE OR STRONGLY AGREE THAT "MY KLC PROGRAM EXPERIENCE IS HELPING ME MAKE MORE PROGRESS ON MY CHALLENGES."

BY LIVING OUT THE KLC'S PRINCIPLES, SETH AND OPEN WICHITA HAVE:

Worked with the city to adopt an open data policy.

Contributed to the reopening of a community jewel — the Lake Afton Public Observatory — by creating a digital media and website campaign for the observatory.

Spawned a group called the ICT Food Circle. It promotes local food vendors and sources through a website and has plans for additional projects.

An advocate for a cause has passion and knowledge, invests his time in learning even more about the cause, mastering the facts and figures, but dedicates only a tiny percentage of time to engaging others and wonders why no one is with him.

The KLC taught Seth the power of giving the work back and creating a trustworthy process. He started thinking about the work of Open Wichita through an adaptive lens. He eventually tried a new tack. Seth identified individuals in the community with the needed abilities and then simply asked them if they were interested in taking part.

What's so hard about that, you might wonder? He just asked them.

But for a guy who had spent most his time behind a computer, coding and cracking — the ultimate technical problem solving — building relationships and engaging others to help solve the problems was a big deal.

It's different work. It's leadership. And it's made all the difference for Open Wichita.

Seth said learning how to keep projects moving forward with a volunteer workforce is the biggest adaptive challenge Open Wichita faces. "That's something I think we're going to struggle with for the rest of our existence," he said.

Except for the city budget project, Seth said, all activities "have a technical (leader) on them that's not me." The more directly he gets involved in an individual project, he said, the more the organization is likely to suffer as a whole.

Seth has learned leadership is an activity. And the activity is about creating a healthy, engaging process that's not reliant on any one individual.

WHAT'S NEXT FOR OPEN WICHITA?

An interactive website that will allow residents to explore the city's budget in depth.

A digital tool listing a schedule of meetings of all public groups. "With the recent political climate, there's been a surge of people interested in being civically engaged," Seth said, adding that there's currently no one place to find all those schedules online. Noting that there's "a ridiculously high number of these" meetings, Seth said the group's main goal is to put them in a format that's easy to navigate.

There's also a proposal — currently being discussed with the Police Department but not yet underway — that would publish information about all police shootings, use-of-force reports and complaints against officers on a website.

KLC PRINCIPLE NO. 1

Leadership is an *activity,* not a *position.*

We often fail this principle on two fronts.

First, we assume leadership isn't for us, or it is only for us based on our title. We let ourselves off the hook if we aren't the person in charge, the person with authority. We are good at being the critic, the Monday-morning quarterback. Or when we do have authority — when we are the CEO, manager, principal, mayor, foreman — we, in a subconscious, self-righteous fashion, shoulder all the responsibility for leading. In doing so, we elevate our importance and cloak it in noble, well-it's-my-job rhetoric.

Second, we engage, we become active, but fail to realize our activity must be focused on creating a healthy process. We are like the politician who gives blustery speeches, but nothing ever actually changes. We are like the advocate — busy, busy, busy with passion and a long to-do list — but the underlying situation remains untouched by progress.

Simply put, confusing leadership and authority is one of the biggest mistakes we can make when trying to lead.

QUESTIONS FOR REFLECTION:

> *What would happen if those in your organization, community or company viewed leadership as an activity, not a position? What would be possible?*
>
> *What would be different for you if you thought of leadership as the activity of mobilizing others to make progress on daunting challenges?*
>
> *What's the process of engagement like in your organization, community or company? What would have to happen for you to help it be a more healthy, inclusive process?*

WHAT HAPPENS WHEN WE TRULY BELIEVE AND LIVE OUT
THE PRINCIPLE "LEADERSHIP IS AN ACTIVITY, NOT A POSITION"?
KLC ALUMS HAVE SOMETHING TO SAY ABOUT THAT.

"There would be more people who would worry less about the position they hold and would concentrate on the issues at hand. They would be more inclusive and include all factions."

BECKY WOLFE
*Andover Area Chamber of Commerce;
Andover, Kansas*

"Empowerment. Progress. It is amazing to watch people who don't just hear this but begin to believe it and what happens to their confidence that they have the power to make a difference within them!"

MARY JANE CHAPMAN
*Facilitator for
Leadership Mitchell County;
Beloit, Kansas*

"People become empowered and positive change results, even from an activity as simple as standing up in a meeting and expressing an idea that would generate a positive result for the common good."

PETER COOK
Leadership Labette; Parsons, Kansas

"The level of creativity and commitment to mission skyrockets."

JULIA FABRIS MCBRIDE
*Kansas Leadership Center;
Wichita, Kansas*

Leadership Principle Nº 2

BATON ROUGE. ST. PAUL. DALLAS.

WHAT HAPPENED IN THOSE THREE CITIES IN THE DAYS
FOLLOWING THE FOURTH OF JULY IN 2016 COULD HAPPEN
ANYWHERE IN AMERICA, INCLUDING KANSAS.

On Tuesday of that week, Alton Sterling died at the hands of police officers in Baton Rouge, Louisiana. I read about it the next day. My heart ached. And then I went on, like most people.

On Wednesday, Philando Castile died at the hands of police officers in St. Paul, Minnesota. The next day, as I waited at a long stoplight in the Kansas City area, I saw on my social media feed the shocking video that showed Mr. Castile dying. It left me sick to my stomach and emotional. Then the light turned green and my thoughts turned, too. Our KLC board of directors' retreat was to start that evening.

Anyone
can lead,
anytime,
anywhere.

The killings didn't become part of our board's discussion that night. They were occasionally on my mind throughout dinner. But we talked about the KLC and listened to the stories of three alumni who had joined us that night.

Alone in my quiet hotel room later, I had trouble sleeping. The deaths kept coming to mind.

When my alarm went off at 5:30 a.m., I checked my phone. Five police officers had been murdered in Dallas. Retribution, according to the gunman.

Baton Rouge. St. Paul. Dallas. The tension between communities of color and law enforcement was immense.

Our board chairman began that day's meeting with a moment of silence for the loss of life in the three communities. We then moved on to discussing the business of the KLC. We took a bus to visit places in Johnson and Wyandotte counties where our alumni were putting KLC ideas to work. The events of that week didn't really come up until lunch.

A half-dozen alums from Kansas City, all African-Americans, had joined the meeting. I don't remember exactly what one of our faculty members said, but she ignited a conversation that mattered.

A collection of black, white, Asian and Hispanic Kansans shared their thoughts and experiences. Black men from Kansas City — KLC alums — shared what it was like to be pulled over by law enforcement officers. White businessmen from mainly white communities asked questions.

A microcosm of Kansas was present. Many backgrounds and professions. Different races and political beliefs. Baton Rouge, St. Paul and Dallas stayed in the middle of the conversation. We explored. We learned. We weren't closer to knowing what, if anything, we could or should do. But the conversation was deep and productively heated.

We then toured some of the most economically depressed neighborhoods in Kansas — just a few minutes away from posh areas of Johnson County.

Discussions continued. The board began contemplating what the KLC could or should do.

By the next morning, an idea had crystalized. The KLC would convene alums to diagnose this situation. It was an adaptive challenge, after all. Everyone has the same goal. No one wants senseless loss of life. But when the goal is the same for almost everyone and progress is still elusive, you know you are dealing with a deep, daunting adaptive challenge.

The KLC continues to convene alums around that issue. We don't play a central part in the debate between communities of color and law enforcement. But we can do something. The KLC has to live out the principle "anyone can lead, anytime, anywhere" too. We can't just preach it. We have to practice it.

There are many valid excuses for the KLC to do nothing on the seemingly intractable nature of the relationship between communities of color and law enforcement: It's not our issue. It's not our job. It could get in the way of other things we are doing. Now is just not the right time. We are in Kansas; those unpleasant events happened in other places.

No, if we believe the principle "anyone can lead, anytime, anywhere," we need to model it.

We have to help people learn that even if they can't do everything, they can usually do something.

A nonprofit might be teetering on the edge of bankruptcy due to fiscal mismanagement by a board and executive director, but the frontline, newly minted social worker can at least do his part to ensure his program is operating efficiently.

A once-proud entrepreneurial company has lost its mojo. Innovation is rare and the CEO is distracted, but the middle manager can still do her part by creating an entrepreneurial culture in her department. She doesn't have authority over everything, but she does over some things.

Partisan gridlock might have overtaken the State Capitol, but Kansans can still reach out in their communities and engage with others who think differently than them.

"ANYONE CAN LEAD, ANYTIME, ANYWHERE" IS PROBABLY THE TOUGHEST KLC PRINCIPLE FOR MOST PEOPLE TO GRASP.

Anyone?

Anytime?

Anywhere?

But we believe it. Anyone can lead, anytime, anywhere.

Rosa Parks sat where she sat on that bus and ignited a movement.

You might not be able to do everything. But you can do something. You can at least lead within your sphere of influence. And here's the thing on deep, daunting, adaptive challenges: No one can fully lead anyway. No one's sphere of influence can reach everyone and everything. The corollary to this principle might be:

No one can fully lead, all the time, everywhere.

Adaptive challenges facing our communities, organizations and companies aren't usually solved by a person. They are solved because enough people — from the top of the organization to the bottom, inside and outside the organization — step up, take risks and exercise leadership.

So yes, anyone can lead, anytime, anywhere. Anyone who has the passion. Anytime that passion moves them. And anywhere they happen to be.

CHARLIE SCHWARZ REMEMBERS THE MOMENT HE DECIDED
TO HELP PLANEVIEW, AN IMPOVERISHED NEIGHBORHOOD
IN WICHITA THAT FOR YEARS HE HAD LITTLE OCCASION TO
VISIT OR EVEN THINK ABOUT.

It was 2009, and Charlie was attending training at the Kansas Leadership
Center with his pastor, the Rev. Jeff Gannon, and several other members of
Chapel Hill Fellowship, a Methodist congregation in affluent east Wichita.
In its search for a project for the common good, the Chapel Hill team visited
Planeview, a dilapidated development containing housing units hurriedly
built in the 1940s to house wartime workers.

Charlie — who had been serving meals to the needy at the Lord's Diner (a nonprofit soup kitchen operated by the Catholic Diocese of Wichita) for years and
had an extensive record of volunteerism and public service — was inspired
but also uninformed.

As Charlie looked around, he saw blighted building after blighted building.
His initial thought was to tear down the ramshackle housing and improve
the neighborhood by taking advantage of government stimulus grants that
existed at the time.

He also thought about his own history with Planeview. As a teenager, he
had driven through with a friend and "caused grief," by purposely making
the car backfire.

Ultimately Jeff, the pastor, challenged his congregation to make a 10-year
commitment to the neighborhood, and Charlie made his own commitment.

81% OF ALUMNI REPORT POSITIVE CHANGE
BECAUSE OF THEIR KLC EXPERIENCE IN REGARD
TO REGULARLY ASKING THEMSELVES, "IS THIS
A TECHNICAL OR ADAPTIVE CHALLENGE?"

"I was very naive to what the needs were."

CHARLIE SCHWARZ
Independent Tax Accountant

Charlie, lanky, gray-haired and soft-spoken, had recently married and undergone heart surgery. When he returned to his accounting job, he found out that his entire division was being eliminated. He was occupying his time by readying his and his wife's previous homes for sale and looking for work.

He talked it over with his wife and decided to make helping Planeview his mission.

Planeview's long decline meant the cost of housing was low, but there are established networks there for new immigrants. It is diverse: The 4,400 residents are 53 percent Hispanic, 22 percent Caucasian, 14 percent Asian and 7 percent African-American. It is also impoverished. About 30 percent of Planeview's 1,300 households live on less than $15,000 a year.

"I was very naive to what the needs were," Charlie said.

But he set about educating himself, recalling his KLC leadership training to take time diagnosing situations.

So Charlie kept asking questions, listening and pondering how to help improve the lives of the residents. He burned through a lot of shoe leather getting to know them. Several joined Chapel Hill's new group, the Planeview Transformation Coalition.

In particular, one Planeview social worker set him straight on his initial idea to tear down the dilapidated houses. In Charlie's view, the homes were an eyesore. But to the people of Planeview, they represented affordable housing. Charlie's idea would take away homes they desperately needed.

He decided to start with what he determined to be low-hanging fruit, something that would fulfill a clear need in the community. But some things are not what they seem, and they ended up testing his perseverance and led to months of sleepless nights.

Charlie decided to build a medical clinic. He thought that building a clinic would help earn the residents' trust.

Charlie was aware of Planeview's reputation as crime- and drug-ridden. His view was that 99 percent of the residents are very giving and hardworking, but they struggle to provide for their families. Many work two or three jobs, and many are without cars, making access to health care difficult.

REV. JEFF GANNON
Senior Pastor, Chapel Hill
United Methodist Church

One day, Charlie had a discussion with folks from Brookside United Methodist Church, Hunter Health Clinic (a safety-net clinic for the poor that operated in shared space with the church) and the city.

It was evident that one area where there was great need — and a great opportunity — was with Hunter Health's Planeview location. The clinic operated out of tight space. There was a physician's assistant but no full-time physician for this community of 4,400.

CHARLIE KEPT ASKING QUESTIONS, LISTENING AND PONDERING HOW TO MAKE PROGRESS. LEADERSHIP ON OUR TOUGHEST CHALLENGES ALMOST ALWAYS REQUIRES THAT APPROACH.

But there was some encouraging news: The clinic had rudimentary plans for an expansion and had secured about $250,000 in federal and state grants.

Charlie was off and running.

He made no outward promises, but he was determined to use his network to help fulfill the need for medical access.

CAROL NAZAR
Program Officer,
Wichita Community Foundation

"I just gave them the freedom to dream a little bigger," Charlie said.

Charlie ultimately was able to persuade both an architectural and an engineering firm to work pro bono on the project. They determined that a new building would be most cost-effective.

The church was willing to set aside space on its property, and Hunter Health was willing to make a 25-year commitment to serving the community.

The next step was securing a contractor and a detailed bid, which came to $600,000.

Numbers and budgets were familiar territory for Charlie. He worked with Hunter Health to whittle that down, scaling back some proposals, and the clinic allocated an additional $100,000 from its grant pool for the project.

Finally, Charlie had his marching orders: He needed to find about $100,000 more. It was now well into 2010. The clinic needed to be built by 2011, or the grants would expire.

To secure that $100,000, Charlie set his sights on a large private foundation in Wichita that he thought was his best and maybe only hope. Charlie submitted the plans for the clinic. The response? A polite but firm no.

For the first time, Charlie was truly flummoxed. "Psychologically, it just set me back," he said.

That type of psychological setback often happens when we attempt to exercise leadership. Mobilizing people to make progress on daunting challenges is a daunting challenge in itself.

A couple of months passed. Charlie felt immense pressure, afraid that his efforts might be viewed like those of fly-by-night organizations that had swooped into Plainview, overpromised and underdelivered. It was November 2010, and he was still in a holding pattern.

He had read something about the Wichita Community Foundation and began to consider another "ask."

He called Carol Nazar, then the Wichita Community Foundation's director of donor and grant-making services. Donors, she said, look for three things:

BY LIVING OUT THE KLC'S PRINCIPLES, CHARLIE AND OTHERS CONNECTED TO PLANEVIEW HAVE:

Built trust in a neighborhood where people had been burned previously. They were used to a group swooping in, promising something big — and maybe even delivering to a degree — and then disappearing.	Helped develop a mission-focused culture in his church.	Engaged residents and benefactors to build something tangible — a new health clinic.

clarity of vision, clear establishment of need and sustainability. "He had all three, right on the head."

Amazingly, Nazar was able to call Charlie fewer than 10 days later with good news: The community foundation board had voted to allocate $40,000 to the clinic proposal, and two private foundations stepped up anonymously to cover the rest.

Construction on the Hunter Health Clinic building was completed in the fall of 2011. For Charlie, both the groundbreaking and the later dedication were thrilling. Planeview residents now have easier access to medical care.

While debates in the State Capitol and in Congress rage on about health care for Americans, Charlie and his team actually got something done on the topic in Plainview.

These days, Charlie has been rebuilding the tax and accounting business that he ran before taking and losing his corporate job. But he isn't done with Planeview.

He and his congregation were serious about their 10-year commitment and their goal to transform lives using their faith.

Today, Methodists, Lutherans and Episcopalians are working together to support a fledgling Spanish-speaking church, Mision San Juan de Dios, inside Brookside United Methodist Church.

"This is where we develop the trust," Charlie said.

The Planeview Transformation Coalition has been folded into a larger missions team at Chapel Hill, and Charlie is still involved. He is most pleased to see dozens of his fellow congregants involved regularly with Planeview and the public elementary school there.

"It's an extremely positive evolution," he said. "It's just so cool to see."

And it never would have happened without Charlie believing that anyone could lead, anytime, anywhere.

WHAT'S NEXT FOR CHARLIE AND CHAPEL HILL?

Continue working with other denominations to support a fledgling Spanish-speaking church in Planeview.

Keep their 10-year promise by continuing to promote and offer volunteer opportunities in Planeview, including at the elementary school.

I CAN'T HELP BUT THINK ABOUT POLITICS WHEN I THINK ABOUT "ANYONE CAN LEAD, ANYTIME, ANYWHERE," OUR SECOND LEADERSHIP PRINCIPLE.

As a former legislator, I love an election as much as anyone. I'm intrigued with races from city hall to the White House. I was a proud dad when, back in 2012, my two third-graders sneaked out of bed so they could watch one of the presidential debates. But as much as I love elections, I also feel that all the focus on the candidates can warp our sense of whom we need to exercise leadership. (Hint: It's not just the politicians. It's us too.)

It can be easy to place an inflated sense of importance on elected officials. Yes, they are important. And their service should be much appreciated. It's important to remember that elected officials have a role in solving tough, daunting challenges, but theirs is not the only role.

On my first day in the Kansas Legislature in 2003, my father sent me the following two lines of poetry from Samuel Johnson:

How small, of all that human hearts endure,
That part which laws or kings can cause or cure.

He was doing his part to help remind me of the limitations of my office. Or conveyed another way, that no one can lead all of the time, everywhere.

Similarly, Paul Tillett, in his 1965 book "The Political Vocation," wrote:

> *Politicians are important to the system, but it is easy to overestimate their capacity to achieve reform. ... They will more likely respond to than suggest far-reaching changes in their environment.*

If Samuel Johnson, Paul Tillett and my father are correct, elected officials can only do so much. Not only can "anyone lead, anytime, anywhere," but if we want progress on the issues most important to our organizations and communities — involving those adaptive challenges — we need to compel more people to lead, more frequently, wherever they can.

FEW HEADS TURNED WHEN BRODERICK CRAWFORD SLIPPED IN UNANNOUNCED AT A MAKESHIFT COLLEGE ARCHITECTURE CLASSROOM IN DOWNTOWN KANSAS CITY, KANSAS.

It was near midterm in 2017, and some University of Kansas students were in the middle of informal presentations about renovation ideas for the Jersey Creek Trail Park. They had joined a massive grassroots effort to turn the deteriorated trail into an inner-city jewel. The students had spent every Friday of the semester meeting in Kansas City with their professor, Shannon Criss. They had biked, walked and explored every nook and cranny of the trail and surrounding parkland that snakes through the northeast part of the city, viewing forgotten playgrounds, a fractured asphalt path and splintered wooden benches.

As Broderick popped in with a guest, students were presenting practical design solutions to address community engagement, zoning challenges and key connection points along the trail.

It was the kind of free exchange of innovative ideas that Broderick and a team of civic-minded community members had dreamed about for years.

"We have multiple individuals, multiple organizations, multiple groups now collaborating with a single voice, with a single purpose, with a single mission — and that's to improve physical activity in this county."

BRODERICK CRAWFORD
Executive Director, New Bethel Church

"I'm elated," said Broderick, executive director of the NBC (New Bethel Church) Community Development Corporation.

Broderick, an alumnus of the Kansas Leadership Center, has invested fully in the principle "anyone can lead, anytime, anywhere."

"We have multiple individuals, multiple organizations, multiple groups now collaborating with a single voice, with a single purpose, with a single mission — and that's to improve physical activity in this county," he said.

Broderick learned early on that he had to inspire others. He had to get others to believe they could lead the community toward better health. It wasn't just the mayor's job or the public health director's job, it was the responsibility of scores of residents. It couldn't be just one church. It couldn't be just one voice. What happens if one person burns out? The group has to mobilize others to accomplish its goal.

It's why NBC is one part of a multifaceted coalition that includes Healthy Communities Wyandotte, the Community Health Council of Wyandotte County, FreeWheels for Kids, the Unified Government Parks and Recreation, the University of Kansas School of Architecture, the Latino Health for All Coalition and others — the list of organizations grows by the week. The organizations are working to improve health in Wyandotte County, which regularly ranks among the worst in the state for health outcomes.

The agencies could have been frustrated that the Unified Government of Wyandotte County and Kansas City, Kansas, hadn't renovated the trail. They also knew the Unified Government didn't have the $1 million-plus for revitalization. Change would start with them. It's why so many agencies are rallying support and awareness.

MONICA MENDEZ
Director, Latino Health
for All Coalition

"All of the awareness will bring a really good outcome," said Monica Mendez, director of the Latino Health for All Coalition.

The students met inside a storefront building that houses Dotte Agency, a multidisciplinary design collaborative that engages neighborhoods to shape the built environment to improve public health. Its architectural ideas alone would save the volunteer renovation group tens of thousands of dollars. It offered several ideas, including the use of stepping stones across the creek as an artful connection. Another suggestion was tall grasses and landscaping to buffer traffic on Parallel Parkway. Other ideas called for more destination points, including a soccer field for children, a sensory garden to draw in residents from the senior housing that sits along the creek and a hillside slide where families could play together.

"Let's get that slide in tomorrow," Broderick said.

Monica and Broderick beamed with pride throughout the presentations.

"Two and a half years ago, Monica and I were sitting in a room wondering what it would look like," Broderick said.

60%

OF ALUMNI REPORT POSITIVE CHANGE BECAUSE OF THEIR KLC EXPERIENCE IN REGARD TO EXPERIMENTING WITH NEW TACTICS TO ADDRESS A CHALLENGE WHEN TRADITIONAL SOLUTIONS ARE INEFFECTIVE.

BY LIVING OUT THE KLC'S PRINCIPLES,
BRODERICK AND OTHERS DETERMINED TO
IMPROVE THE HEALTH OF WYANDOTTE COUNTY HAVE:

Started a massive grassroots effort that has engaged diverse voices to advance the cause of renovating the Jersey Creek Trail Park.

Developed walking clubs and reached out to churches, a retirement home and other neighbors to hear their hopes and dreams for the trail.

Gained the attention of city officials, who included the grassroots group on a discussion about nearby pedestrian crosswalks.

Praised governmental and private groups that have updated some playgrounds.

Again and again students proposed ways to resolve challenges that had frustrated community members for decades. The park, they pointed out repeatedly, has few direct connections to their main customers — adjoining churches and residential property. The sidewalks don't connect. There are few crosswalks and several broken streetlights that make public safety a concern.

"The second it starts to get dark, it starts to get a little eerie," observed one student.

Some of those problems are easy to fix.

"It might be good to have a civic walkabout," said Shannon, the professor.

Broderick immediately set to work to make it all happen.

Back at the trail, Broderick shows off the tangible changes.

SHANNON CRISS
Associate Professor and Registered Architect,
University of Kansas School of Architecture,
Design and Planning

Mount Carmel Church built a new playground along the trail. Mile marker signs were installed to let bikers and walkers log activity. A historic footbridge has been cleared of dense brush that once hid it from view. And a trail counter was installed so the renovation team can count users to measure their progress.

At Mac's Park, a pocket park along the trail, the Unified Government installed new playground equipment and will add a full-size basketball court and a shelter house offering families space for birthdays, reunions and picnics. A walking path will also be constructed along the perimeter of the park.

The best part, Broderick said, is that the path will have a crosswalk to connect it properly with the Jersey Creek Trail Park.

"I would like to believe that it's because of the community efforts," he said.

Broderick doubts the crosswalk connection would have been on anyone's radar a few years earlier. It's a sign that the renovation team is rounding a corner. The local government is taking notice.

Remember, elected officials rarely lead. They follow. They quickly become experts in knowing exactly what the public expects of them and their survival depends on meeting those expectations. Broderick got their attention.

Broderick had long said that if they were successful, then state and national groups of all political persuasions would flock there to learn from their work — efforts that transcend politics. "Ideology does not dictate health, so it doesn't matter on what side of the aisle you sit," he said. "Health still affects us both equally."

Thankfully for Wyandotte County, a movement was launched that embraced the belief that anyone can lead, anytime, anywhere.

WHAT'S NEXT FOR NBC (NEW BETHEL CHURCH) COMMUNITY DEVELOPMENT CORPORATION?

> *Continue to build momentum by encouraging community members to use the trail before going to the Unified Government to ask for more money.*

> *Monitor trail use with an electronic device to gauge progress.*

> *Improve sidewalk access to the park for residential areas surrounding the park.*

> *Encourage civic leaders to review and implement the ideas put forth by University of Kansas students.*

KLC PRINCIPLE NO. 2

Anyone can lead, *anytime, anywhere.*

This principle is hard to live out, because we often look for the quickest and easiest excuse not to lead: I'm not the right person. It's not the right time. It's not the right place.

To bring forth a Kansas for tomorrow, this mindset must fade from our consciousness.

Gone are the days when a small, exclusive group of individuals (usually wealthy, white males) served as unofficial "city fathers." Leadership and power is being distributed. Anyone can lead, anytime, anywhere.

QUESTIONS FOR REFLECTION:

What would happen if those in your organization, community or company believed anyone could lead, anytime, anywhere? What would be possible?

What would be different for you personally if you embraced this principle?

Who is expected to exercise leadership in your organization, community or company? When are they expected to lead? Where are they expected to lead? How close or how far is your organization to living out the principle that anyone can lead, anytime, anywhere?

WHAT HAPPENS WHEN WE TRULY BELIEVE AND LIVE OUT
THE PRINCIPLE "ANYONE CAN LEAD, ANYTIME, ANYWHERE"?
KLC ALUMS HAVE SOMETHING TO SAY ABOUT THAT.

"Fresh and new perspectives! Energized and
passionate hearts/mindsets. Endless possibilities."

ADRION ROBERSON
DESTINY! Bible Fellowship Community Church; Kansas City, Kansas

"Unusual voices and people who would never
have engaged in leadership development start
to engage with these ideas."

TIM STEFFENSMEIER
Kansas State University; Manhattan, Kansas

"Everyone in the organization feels valued
and is not only willing to contribute their time,
talent and expertise, but also deliver at levels
much higher than you can usually imagine."

NICOLE PFANNENSTIEL
Sunflower Electric Power Corp.; Hays, Kansas

Leadership Principle
N°3

"BOB, WHY ARE YOU WALKING?" THEY ASKED. BOB ANSWERED,
"I WANT THEM TO KNOW WE ARE WALKING WITH THEM."

"You mean you are walking for them. Walking to raise money or something
for these poor people?" they replied.

"No, I walk with them, not for them," Bob answered as he described his
1994 walk from Kansas City, Kansas to Guatemala and his 2011 walk from
Guatemala to Chile.

In the 1980s, my great uncle Bob Hentzen; another great uncle Bud Hentzen
of Wichita; and my grandmother Nadine Hentzen Pearce of Leawood started
a wonderful effort to help the poorest of the world's poor. Called Unbound and
located in a warehouse in Kansas City, Kansas, the effort now delivers more

than $100 million annually to help the poor around the world. Bob has passed away, but his spirit of walking with, not for, is imbedded in the organization. And I think that idea is in the same spirit as our leadership principle "it starts with you and must engage others."

Leadership is mobilizing others to make progress on daunting challenges. It is not mobilizing yourself to do everything for others.

The world is too full of passionate advocates — for social issues, for new products, for religious conversion — who are unskilled at mobilizing anyone to do anything. Fortunately, Kansas is becoming full of people who actually have the skills and seize the opportunities to mobilize others. Leadership isn't just about you being passionate. It's about you engaging others, tapping into their passions and collectively fostering progress. You have to walk with them.

Bob, Nadine and Bud weren't satisfied with simply being passionate advocates for the poor. They engaged others, and that engagement has made all the difference. The effort lives on without them. Thousands of people are involved. They didn't just engage donors. They engaged the poor and have empowered them to help direct and guide the organization and how it uses its financial resources. The $100 million a year comes in from $20 and $30 contributions, not from million-dollar donors.

Whether it's in regard to global poverty or organizational life, leadership is about engaging others to make progress. This chapter explores what it looks like to hold dear the leadership principle "it starts with you and must engage others."

WHEN A CENTURY-OLD ORGANIZATION SEEMS TO BE LOSING ITS RELEVANCE, IT'S SCARY TO THINK THAT IT COULD FADE AWAY. BUT IT CAN BE EVEN SCARIER TO CHANGE WHEN ITS CULTURE IS RICH WITH TRADITION.

That's the challenge Kansas 4-H Youth Development was facing in the early 2000s. The organization is a national program run by land-grant universities.

A pillar of rural life for decades, 4-H once was the go-to organization to help kids learn how to be engaged, active members of our rural communities.

Membership and volunteerism with 4-H has been plummeting in Kansas and elsewhere — yet another symptom of the decline of small-town and rural America. Some 4-H leaders, such as Rhonda Atkinson, now associate director of the Kansas 4-H Foundation, took this as a warning: Adapt or perish. That was the problem she wanted to solve when she joined a Kansas Leadership Center program in 2008.

In the process, Rhonda and other 4-H faithful soon found themselves wrestling over the very identity of 4-H.

In a traditional 4-H community club, children and teens choose a project to work on over the course of a year. Originally based around agriculture and homemaking, these projects grew to include subjects like photography,

WRESTLING ADAPTIVE CHALLENGES OFTEN REQUIRES US TO WRESTLE OURSELVES, OUR IDENTITY, OUR PREFERENCES. WE CONTRIBUTE TO THE EXISTENCE OF THE CHALLENGE, AND FACING THAT REALITY IS NEVER EASY. KANSAS 4-H IS LEARNING THIS FIRSTHAND. TWO HYPOTHETICAL EXAMPLES:

University faculty members are concerned their institution is no longer the bastion of free speech it once was, but are unaware that their own implicit bias contributes to quashing students' willingness to share contrary opinions.

An organization needs growth but is stagnant. Employees fail to realize that their comfort with how things work (which is leading to stagnation) is the real barrier to growth.

"We believe that by spreading the KLC training, we're building our capacity. We just put the KLC principles and competencies in a 4-H context."

RHONDA ATKINSON
Associate Director, Kansas 4-H Foundation

crafts, rocketry and more. Whole families would attend meetings as faithfully as they went to church. Parents volunteered as leaders. That interaction is the true purpose of the program, 4-H leaders say — and always will be.

"The point is working with an adult and with their peers. That's the magic of 4-H," Rhonda said.

As 4-H slips from prominence, so does that magic. Embracing the it-starts-with-you-and-must-engage-others principle, Rhonda began experimenting to engage others in the work of redefining, or perhaps simply saving, 4-H. Her task wouldn't be to solve the future of 4-H but to mobilize enough others to invest their time and energy to solve the future of 4-H.

In 2012, that experimentation led to the Kansas 4-H Foundation's launch of the Growing Kansas Leaders program. Extension agents, the "boots on the ground" for land-grant institutions and 4-H, were tasked with innovating to reach a new generation of 4-H'ers. Each agent drafted a three-year business plan, with KLC guidance, that included programming ideas and goals for growing membership and volunteers.

A radical idea emerged. Some opted to try short-term programs to give new members and volunteers a different point of entry to the 4-H world. These special interest clubs, or SPIN Clubs, were a huge departure from 4-H culture, and the agents in the pilot program risked the confidence of their longtime supporters to try them — especially when a lot of people weren't convinced that anything needed to be fixed.

Kansas 4-H is like any organization or system. Change is hard. The way things had been operating worked for most people, or at least appeared to work. Progress on adaptive challenges requires us to do something different. Maybe you are a part of an established institution like 4-H, or maybe you are in a young organization that is developing habits and "the way we do things." Leadership on adaptive challenges requires us to buck the system and mobilize others to do so, too. Suggesting change for a youth-development organization might not sound like a big deal, but if you were inside that organization and had years of history doing things a certain way, what Rhonda was encouraging could be seen as concerning or just unnecessary.

"In some cases, they say, 'It's not a problem; we're good,'" Rhonda said. "But then you look at the number of young people who don't have the opportunity to participate in that community club work over a 12-year span. That's where we tried to add in some new tools."

Data doesn't lie. And the data suggested change was needed.

SPIN Clubs usually meet for six weeks. Each club has a focus, many in the STEM fields: science, technology, engineering and math. In Seward County, one of the first clubs introduced kids to crime-scene investigation. A beekeeping club in Dickinson County partnered with a retirement community for a multigenerational experience. Like their counterparts in community clubs, SPIN Club members must demonstrate what they have learned through projects that they can enter in county and state fairs.

As one agent in the pilot program put it, the SPIN Clubs are "an addition, not a subtraction." But to many longtime members, it just didn't feel like 4-H. It felt like another loss.

Five years in, Rhonda thinks the needle has moved — slowly.

The first group of extension agents completed the pilot program in 2015. The last group finished in 2017. Atkinson said most of the participants made progress on their overall goals, which included:

25 percent growth in 4-H youth membership.

15 percent increase in traditional community club membership.

20 percent increase in volunteer participation.

It's risky to ask a culture to change, even for its own survival. But the believers in this new approach to 4-H are pressing forward with lessons learned in mind. "We have a lot of work just to get the concept out to others in the state," Rhonda said. "We are looking at how to take what we've learned, reshape it and offer it to other counties. I think that's where we're headed."

Eventually the magic of 4-H, and what it does for community engagement and youth development, just might be preserved and strengthened.

RON ALEXANDER
Teacher,
Kansas Leadership Center

KLC faculty member Ron Alexander, who has long been involved in 4-H, facilitated community meetings at the start of the process to help people work through hard questions and reactions to the proposed changes.

71% OF ALUMNI CAN NAME AT LEAST THREE OTHER KLC ALUMNI THEY CAN TURN TO FOR HELP WITH MAKING PROGRESS ON THEIR CHALLENGES.

BY LIVING OUT THE KLC'S PRINCIPLES, RHONDA AND 4-H HAVE:

Coached extension agents in 15 counties on leadership with the Growing Kansas Leaders pilot program, which also helped many counties grow their 4-H membership and volunteer pools.

Created alternative opportunities for more young people to have a 4-H experience, even if it's outside the traditional model, such as SPIN Clubs.

Guided difficult conversations in small towns and rural communities about the changing face of 4-H in the 21st century.

Recruited dozens of new adult volunteers into 4-H to share their expertise with youth in their communities.

WHAT'S NEXT FOR KANSAS 4-H?

Expand the Growing Kansas Leaders program to extension agents statewide.

Help more local 4-H clubs connect with community partners, such as libraries, to reach more young people and offer more robust programming.

Offer free leadership training to adult 4-H volunteers, made possible by a grant from the Kansas 4-H Foundation. "We put the KLC principles and competencies in a 4-H context," said Rhonda, associate director for the foundation, which raises money to support the state's 4-H organization.

EMBRACING THE PRINCIPLE

It starts with you and must *engage others.*

BY MARK MCCORMICK
KLC alum, friend and community thought leader

I rose early that morning in 2009 to embark on a new world. For roughly 26 of my then 41 years I'd wanted nothing else but the life I led as a journalist, but when the latest corporate downsizing left me with no other choice, I climbed into a dinghy and, tossing in the economic chop, paddled for the unfamiliar shoreline of a new career.

This new world at The Kansas African American Museum would consist of silver gelatin prints, original lithographs and graphite on paper. And there were dehumidifiers, acid-free paper and watercolors embellished with pen and ink. I knew nothing about what humidity or light did to art. I'd never worked with a board of directors. I had no familiarity with facility management, fundraising or grant writing.

Still, most people welcomed me. My reputation as a trusted local opinion leader seemed to bring the museum sorely needed credibility. I consciously tried to exude a competence and confidence I did not possess. I had to, considering the challenges.

I'd inherited an African-American museum surrounded by a county jail full of African-Americans. The museum had a pronounced public relations problem that I had helped create as a newspaper columnist critical of some curious expenditures. Upon learning I'd been selected to lead the museum, critics — most of whom weren't museum members — declared me unfit. I would face the city government's notoriously tough Cultural Funding Committee in two weeks. A protest on the museum's front steps — with media on hand — aimed at the museum's board and me, surfaced my first week. And on my first morning after I had risen early to get a head start on the day, I realized after arriving and walking up the steps that I didn't yet have a key to the building.

I would learn in the intervening weeks and months following my program with the Kansas Leadership Center that I faced a classic adaptive challenge — a quandary requiring deep and patient learning, one in which I would make progress rather than find a solution. I would also come to understand that, but for the Kansas Leadership Center, the museum might not now, eight years later, have achieved a string of balanced budgets, enjoyed an improved public image and be engaged in a monumental plan for a capital campaign. I think of KLC ideas less as theories and more as the set of keys I needed on my first morning not only to enter the building, but also to access its hidden potential.

My first inkling of this surfaced in the coaching pairings offered at the close of the KLC program. At the time, I didn't want a coach. I was just too busy. It felt like an imposition.

Boy, was I wrong.

My meetings with Carlota Ponds, and later with Greg Meissen, addressed my initial crisis of confidence. I seemed busy but unproductive. Scattered. Carlota and Greg helped me find my can-do attitude, helped me better understand what triggered me as well as recognize my tendency to engage in busywork to avoid tougher, more complicated work.

CARLOTA PONDS
Director of International Student Services, Hesston College

Their coaching, more importantly, applied theories to actual situations and gave me a deeper knowledge of competencies than I would have had otherwise. Dispassionate, classroom, ivory-tower discussions were one thing, but I was almost immediately applying these principles and competencies under intense pressure and scrutiny.

So I sought a meeting with the museum's harshest critics, people I had rarely heard from but who had burst into a board meeting once and demanded stacks of financial documents.

I brought the documents and offered explanations. I invited them to future meetings. I gave out my cell phone number. I apologized on behalf of the institution for not communicating better. I laid bare my challenge, a six-figure deficit, and my vision — financial recovery, then a capital campaign for a new museum.

Before long, many of those detractors sought volunteer opportunities with us. One agreed to lead one-on-one genealogy sessions for every new member who joined. Another, a school principal, partnered with us on youth events. Another joined my board.

MARK MCCORMICK ENGAGED HIS HARSHEST CRITICS, NOT TO DEBATE BUT TO DISCUSS. LEADERSHIP ON OUR TOUGHEST CHALLENGES REQUIRES US TO ENGAGE OTHERS — INCLUDING, AND PERHAPS ESPECIALLY — OUR LOUDEST DETRACTORS.

That exterior work preceded interior work with an alternately heroic and disengaged board.

The board seemed at its best in times of crisis, rallying to keep the museum afloat. But exhausted after such prolonged efforts, it often fell back to rest and reflect.

I feared that my running such a smooth ship kept them operating at the margins. So as existing board members rolled off and new ones joined, I worked to raise engagement expectations, most specifically board giving and committee service.

Board members eventually voted unanimously to be personally invoiced for amounts below what they had pledged to raise, an innovation among local nonprofit organizations. In 2016, they contributed nearly $40,000. Prior to my arrival, board members rarely gave anything. Each board member also joined two museum committees.

Board engagement is much better now. Members have a greater sense of purpose and have actively embraced our latest push for a capital campaign to finance a new building.

Things aren't perfect.

That $40,000 should have been about $48,000, and while some committees meet regularly, others barely convene.

But we've come a long way.

Learning how best to intervene, how to engage unusual voices and convince them, by speaking directly from my heart to their sense of loss, that I was sincerely trying to create a process of engagement that they could trust greatly helped our public image with our core constituents.

GREG MEISSEN
Professor,
Wichita State University

Raising the heat with the board and infusing their work with purpose has helped put some frustrating board dysfunction behind us.

I now have the ring of keys I needed on my first day, even one that opens the door of possibilities.

I have arrived some mornings to find diapers in our hedge, left behind by women visiting the jail with children in tow. I've found tiny socks on the sidewalk along with dropped pacifiers.

During hot summers, our steps have offered the only bit of shade for those who are newly released, and in the bitter cold of winter, they have huddled on the north side of the building, hiding from clawing winds.

But as important as it may have been to see things precisely as they were at the museum, I also needed to see things differently, as they could be.

A child stopped me one evening as I was locking up. She appeared to have just left the jail with her mother. She'd been running up and down the steps and hugging the 30-foot columns out front when she saw me and asked sweetly and innocently, "Is this your castle?"

I smiled involuntarily and said, "Actually sweetheart, it's yours."

She beamed as her mom shot me a pleasant smirk, grabbed the child's hand and led her down the sidewalk to a car. I could hear the child asking plaintively, "Will you bring me back later to see my castle?"

I realized then that finally I'd reached the shore.

It wasn't a new world necessarily, but the same world seen with greater depth and clarity through a new lens.

A KLC lens.

BY LIVING OUT THE KLC'S PRINCIPLES, MARK
AND THE KANSAS AFRICAN AMERICAN MUSEUM HAVE:

Turned around a moribund nonprofit organization.

Learned how to untangle adaptive challenges from technical problems and address each appropriately.

Created new ways to motivate a fatigued board of directors.

WHAT'S NEXT FOR MARK AND THE MUSEUM?

Continue to build on their successes and continue to build membership.

Expose more members of the organization — staff as well as the board of directors — to KLC principles.

ONE OF THE BIGGEST BARRIERS TO ENGAGING OTHERS
IS THE DREADED "SILO MENTALITY."

The KLC works with a number of organizations, and each is concerned with their people's inability to engage beyond their silo, to get beyond their way of thinking or their faction.

"We must break people out of their silos!"

"Our silo mentality is stifling our innovation."

Or my favorite: "We prefer the term 'silicones of excellence,' rather than silos, but regardless they are getting in the way."

The danger of silo thinking is obvious. People fail to see the whole picture, missing out on crucial data needed to solve tough challenges. Others fail to be exposed to others' thinking and data, which keeps them from seeing the whole picture.

Silo thinking is so dangerous that we are often asked to work with organizations for the primary purpose of helping people learn how to exercise leadership to knock the silos down.

What's true in our organizations is also true in our civic life. Our silo thinking threatens everything.

We live in liberal and conservative silos, rich and poor silos, rural and urban silos, university-educated and high school-educated silos.

Much like the CEO who knows that silo thinking threatens her company, silo thinking in our society threatens everything we care about.

Our children's education, roads, tax structure, economic policies and safety-net duties all suffer.

Like the CEO who realizes that unless marketing and production get on the same page, the company is doomed, our silo living — our division — is now so bad that division itself is an issue.

Why do all these silos exist in our society? Cultural anthropologists will explain it to us someday. I can only assume it has something to do with technology giving us the ability to isolate ourselves. I also assume it will take a generation or more to bring us back to a less divided society. So for the time being, working across these silos — factions — or working to bring together those who are divided is a necessity. It is part of the work of leadership. It might be *the* work of leadership.

Will everyone hold hands and be on the same page? Of course not. Civic life is rough and tough, and it's not for the faint of heart. One-hundred percent consensus is rarely possible. But winning issues with your faction alone isn't sustainable. If it's adaptive work, other points of view — other silos — have information and ideas needed for defining the problem and imagining the solutions.

What do we do about it? My answer comes from the prayer of St. Francis of Assisi: "Lord, make me an instrument of your peace." I read that to mean: "Help me bridge the divides."

And the way to be an instrument of peace is described later in the prayer: "Grant that I may not so much seek to be consoled as to console, to be understood as to understand."

Breaking down the silos, decreasing our division, is a paramount issue for leadership. Progress will be made when we quit defending our silo, when we quit trying to get others to understand our silo, and when we start consoling and understanding others. My experience tells me that when we do that, we receive the same in return. And then the silos are a little lower, we are less divided and we can make progress.

Leadership starts with you and must engage others, from different factions and different perspectives.

KLC PRINCIPLE NO. 3

It starts with you and must *engage others.*

Mark engaged his toughest critics. Rhonda engaged her network in the field. My great uncle Bob engaged the poor. And in doing so, progress was made on tough challenges.

We want to believe we can make progress on daunting challenges without engaging others. Yet every time we make that assumption, we help the challenge persist. It's not enough for an individual to have passion for a cause. On tough challenges it's not even enough to have passion and deep knowledge or expertise. Adaptive challenges are solved by mobilizing others to take up the work. When we lead on adaptive challenges, our effort needs to stir something in others, to fan the flames of their engagement.

QUESTIONS FOR REFLECTION:

Who do you need to be engaged with to make progress on your organization's or community's toughest challenges?

What would be different if more people in your organization or community thought of leadership as needing to start with you, but required you to engage others?

What's the process of engagement like in your organization, community or company? What would have to happen for you to help it be a more healthy, inclusive process?

WHAT HAPPENS WHEN WE TRULY BELIEVE AND LIVE OUT
THE PRINCIPLE "IT STARTS WITH YOU AND MUST ENGAGE OTHERS"?
KLC ALUMS HAVE SOMETHING TO SAY ABOUT THAT.

"One important thing that I have learned from KLC is that I am far more effective as a director if I make sure that all of our volunteers feel a part of what we are doing and are totally engaged in the outcome."

SUE HACK
Leadership Lawrence, The Chamber of Lawrence; Lawrence, Kansas

"We would have fewer individuals who burn out on projects because they took on too much. We would also have fewer individuals who felt lonely while trying to work on challenges."

LALO MUNOZ
El Centro of Topeka; Topeka, Kansas

"We resist becoming another 'self-help' organization and engage in the innovative work of developing people to make progress in a networked world."

TIM STEFFENSMEIER
Kansas State University; Manhattan, Kansas

Leadership Principle
Nº 4

I WAS TRAVELING FROM SOME PLACE OUT EAST BACK TO
KANSAS IN 2013. AT A LAYOVER, I STOPPED IN AN AIRPORT
BOOKSTORE. ONE IMPULSE BUY LATER, I WAS WALKING
TOWARD MY GATE WITH A COPY OF KEN SEGALL'S "INSANELY
SIMPLE: THE OBSESSION THAT DRIVES APPLE'S SUCCESS."

A recent convert to the Apple fan club, I had been intrigued by Apple CEO
Steve Jobs ever since I read a biography of him. I assumed Segall's book
would be an interesting read about a company that intrigued me. It was
that and more.

Your purpose must be clear.

I knew it would be good when I opened the cover and saw a quote from Henry David Thoreau (his book "Walden" had a big impact on me in college):

"Simplify! Simplify!"

And just under that quote was another from Jobs:

"Simplify!"

Why did Thoreau go to Walden? He wrote: "I went to the woods because I wished to live deliberately, to front only the essential facts of life, and see if I could not learn what it had to teach, and not, when I came to die, discover that I had not lived." Thoreau sought simplicity to help him find his purpose.

Jobs took that same notion beyond just himself and built one of the most successful organizations in history around it.

The idea of simplicity has always intrigued me. My dad, a former journalist, used to edit my school papers and would always start with a chat about "culling unnecessary words." My good friend Bill Peterson — a smart man with degrees from the University of Michigan and DePaul University — likes to say, "Explain it to me like I'm a third-grader." Friend and mentor Marty Linsky said, "Simplicity is the flip side of complexity. ... You've got to push through complexity and make it simple." My sister Clare, a successful artist and designer, helps me appreciate the simplicity of white space in design and tells me, "Less is more."

Segall's book isn't really about Apple, but instead about what happens when an organization is clear about purpose.

More and more Kansans are clear about purpose due to their engagement with the Kansas Leadership Center. And that clarity is leading to more successful Kansas companies, communities and organizations.

Reading the book on the flight back, I came across a story about Jobs — upon his return as CEO after being forced out — convening a gathering of Apple employees for a pivotal announcement. He said Apple would immediately reduce its product line from dozens of items to four. Everything else would be eliminated.

Apple had the smarts to create all those products, but to do something truly special — to transform how people live, work and play — Apple would need to focus.

Just because we can do something doesn't mean we should. How many of our organizations are stretched too thin, doing too many things — and none of them as well as they could or should be done? How often could we say the same thing about ourselves?

I stopped reading after that story, grabbed a pen and paper, and started imagining what it would look like for the KLC to "simplify" in a similar way. At the time, the KLC had something like 27 programs, each for a specific audience or subaudience. I know, complex. I scribbled some notes but couldn't figure it out. Simplicity was elusive!

Fast forward several months, and Ken Segall was speaking to a group of 200 Kansans in KLC's Konza Town Hall. He told the same story. And again I got out my paper. Complexity, complexity, complexity! Simplicity is hard.

I began to realize that simplicity is harder than complexity. Smug, smart people often feel satisfied when they can understand something very complex. But truly smart people grasp complex things and make them simple. "Explain it to me like I'm a third-grader."

It took some time and lots of conversations, but the KLC's version of "simplicity" emerged. Twenty-seven programs were boiled down to just three. It would significantly rock the KLC boat, something that tends to happen when you are clear about your purpose. But KLC faculty, staff and board members believed it would make us stronger. It has. Our purpose is clearer.

Sometimes it's hard to learn your own lessons. It can be hard to practice what you preach. KLC's principle "your purpose must be clear" is on banners and materials throughout the Kansas Leadership Center, but our battle with complexity/simplicity — our battle with getting clear about our own purpose and how to actualize it — was still a battle.

My experience tells me it's hard to stay on purpose. Distractions abound. Intentional and unintentional efforts by others can quickly knock us off purpose. The hustle and bustle, the complexity of life gets in the way, which contributes to why leadership is so rare.

Leadership and purpose go hand in hand. It's hard to get clear about purpose, whether it's your individual purpose or an organization's purpose. This chapter tells two stories involving KLC alums. The first is about an individual who gets clear about her own purpose, a self-discovery journey common among thousands of Kansans who have come through KLC training. The second is a story about an organization getting clearer about purpose and aligning efforts accordingly, also common among many organizations that connect with the KLC.

FOR ALL OF THE KANSAS LEADERSHIP CENTER'S WORK WITH GROUPS, ITS CONVENING OF ORGANIZATIONS FROM ACROSS THE STATE AND ITS CONFERENCES IN ITS STADIUM AUDITORIUM, THE GREATEST MANIFESTATIONS OF ITS WORK MAY BE THE INDIVIDUALS IT HAS INFLUENCED FOR THE BETTER:

People who have taken a journey of 1,000 steps inside their own minds and inside their own hearts to help discover or clarify their purpose.

This certainly appears to be the journey Christina Long took while engaging with the KLC.

Christina said she'd hit a wall.

"I'm really good about talking around my problems to where they sound positive. And she (Sylvia Robinson, certified Kansas Leadership Center coach) made me cut straight to the chase. And stripped me down to truth."

CHRISTINA LONG
Owner/Principal Consultant, CML Collective

She'd been adept at so many things for so long in her life. She could read by age 3. She excelled in school. She launched her journalism career at a midsized metro, a respected newspaper that people worked for years trying to reach.

Successful there, she took a job at one of the nation's largest school districts, helping families stay better engaged with their children's schooling. But in a span of months her department collapsed from a robust 24 members to one, and she was that one.

That was the moment of impact not only in regard to her career but about the nobly interpreted story she'd always told herself about her purpose. The way forward, which had always been so clear, had grown foggy. That's where her frenetic drive hit a wall. She no longer was clear on purpose and using it to propel her to great success.

But strangely, the moment was less about her work with families and schools and more about her budding relationship with her coach and her relationship with herself.

"For me, a turning point was the mentoring conversation that I had with Sylvia," Christina explained. Sylvia Robinson is a certified Kansas Leadership Center coach. Long said, "I'm really good about talking around my problems to where they sound positive. And she made me cut straight to the chase. And stripped me down to truth. And in that moment of truth, during the coaching conversation, she helped me to understand that I brought more value to Wichita outside of the school district.

"That was a tough conversation. There were tears."

Today, because her coach cut her "to the core as precisely as she did," a new Christina has been unleashed. She runs her own company, helps others start their own businesses and does much more.

"KLC made me a better person," she said. "I was able to be a better Christina as I launched my company. That was also just kind of another indication that, yeah, I could possibly make this leap and be successful in it.

"It helped prompt me because of the relationship I developed with my coach, the relationship I had with my coach during a critical point of my life that has allowed me to see beyond the district and to be able to go further into my career and break away from the district. And my career, being my own boss, having my own business."

Now, she and her husband (Jonathan, who was featured in Chapter 1. Yes, they are a power couple.) hope to do for others what the KLC did for them.

"The coaching I received spoke to me directly," she said, "from KLC staff members from the front desk to the second floor. They were there for me at a critical moment when I was feeling so overwhelmed and so undervalued and overworked and underappreciated. My emotions were very raw."

But there was a specific slide in a PowerPoint presentation her coach showed her that made all of the difference. It was a quotation simply presented in black type on a plain white background.

SYLVIA ROBINSON
Certified KLC Coach

"It said, 'The inside of the comfort zone might be a beautiful place, but nothing grows there.'"

Christina's clarity about purpose is a story that could be recounted by countless Kansans. We can't lead if we aren't clear on our own individual purpose.

That goes for our organizations, too. Organizations struggle to get clear about purpose in the same way individuals do. Just as our lives get busy with distractions left and right, organizational life becomes all-consuming, and it often seems an organization's purpose is simply to keep up with the crazy busy pace of running an organization.

BY LIVING OUT THE KLC'S PRINCIPLES, CHRISTINA HAS:

Peeled away at her layers to discover her true purpose.

Launched her own business and become her own boss.

WHAT'S NEXT FOR CHRISTINA LONG?

Pay it forward to others looking to follow their true purpose.

MCPHERSON COLLEGE IN CENTRAL KANSAS IS ONE OF THOSE ORGANIZATIONS THAT HAS BECOME CLEAR ON PURPOSE. IT IS PIONEERING A BLEND OF LIBERAL ARTS AND ENTREPRENEURSHIP THAT TREATS INNOVATION AS AN ESSENTIAL ELEMENT OF HIGHER EDUCATION AND STUDENT LIFE.

Rather than slotting a few business classes into an existing curriculum, it's using entrepreneurship to lift up liberal arts — the college's purpose — and keep it relevant in our tech-forward culture and marketplace. Enrollment, job placement and graduate school attendance are all going up.

Why? In 2010, McPherson College began offering students money to develop their own business ideas. Cash and college students are a winning formula, so it wasn't a surprise when the Horizon Fund, as it is called, was a hit.

The surprise came when faculty members latched on to the entrepreneurial mindset. As a result, they are transforming their campus and their curriculum for the 21st century.

"We've had great luck infusing this into areas to benefit students," said college President Michael Schneider. "But the biggest impact to entrepreneurship on campus has been with the faculty. That's what is sustainable.

"The surprise is that the faculty continue to get excited about being more entrepreneurial and finding more ways to empower their students."

Michael, a 1996 McPherson College graduate, worked in startup businesses before returning to his alma mater in 2002. Seven years later, still in his 30s, Michael became one of the nation's youngest college presidents.

Early on, Michael said he was frustrated by the college's struggle to retain students. Then, through the Kansas Leadership Center, he realized he was trying to solve an adaptive challenge with a technical approach. "That was an important moment in the evolution of how I think about leading an institution, whether it's a business or a college," Michael said.

"Higher education is all about not making any mistakes. It's not very forgiving. But this has given us a framework for faculty to try different things. Because it's out of the president's office, we say, 'Try this, and if it doesn't work, it's OK.'"

MICHAEL SCHNEIDER
President, McPherson College

He wanted to introduce liberal arts students to the traits of entrepreneurship and give them a safe space to experiment, to fail and to try again. Michael talked to his faculty and staff about his idea, and he listened. He asked them to draft their own definitions of entrepreneurship across the curriculum. With their input, the college created the Transformative Entrepreneurship minor and programs like the Horizon Fund. The fund offers grants of up to $500 to students who successfully pitch an original entrepreneurial idea that offers value to the community.

Faculty members started to weave the concepts of creativity, innovation and perseverance into their liberal arts courses. In response, the college created the Horizon Faculty Fellowship, which provides resources to incorporate entrepreneurial concepts into an existing class or start a new one. Half of the college's faculty has completed the program.

"There's been this shift from focusing on students and student programming to faculty," Michael said.

As a result, McPherson College faculty members are empowered to take calculated risks in the classroom, and the whole campus has been energized. "Higher education is all about not making any mistakes. It's not very forgiving," Michael said. "But this has given us a framework for faculty to try different things. Because it's out of the president's office, we say, 'Try this, and if it doesn't work, it's OK.'"

Some of their small, liberal arts peers don't grasp what McPherson College is doing. But others have taken notice. In 2015 and 2016, McPherson College was the only Kansas institution named a Great College to Work For by The Chronicle of Higher Education. In 2016, it was the second-highest ranked Kansas school on the annual U.S. News & World Report Best Colleges list for the Midwest region.

The recognition is great, and the college isn't stopping there. In 2016, Michael embarked on another listening tour to create a strategic plan to set new milestones based on a shared vision. "Instead of planning by committee, we planned by community," he said. "We wanted to create a document that people could find themselves in."

The "community by design" process focused on growth, modeled after the college's successful, unique automotive restoration program; developing entrepreneurial faculty; nurturing facilities that support growth; and building a $1 billion endowment.

The plan features a framework called the Enterprising MC Student that calls for career-focused experiences through internships, field experiences and service learning. For its part, the visual arts department created a joint digital media major with the communications department. Faculty members sought a design firm partner to give students real-life agency experience. And the student-run design firm, ETCH, became central to the curriculum.

The data on McPherson College's experiment are promising. Enrollment is about 700, up about 20 percent since entrepreneurship became part of the landscape. Retention is up, too, as Michael had hoped. He's especially proud that nearly all liberal arts graduates are getting placed in a job in their field, graduate school or service work.

"It gets back to adaptive work. (Entrepreneurship) is a tool we can all use and think things through together. It's not a program, it's a mindset — a way to go about doing things. It's evolving, and that makes it hard to market and explain. The bottom line is: It's making us better." That happens when we get clear on purpose.

BY LIVING OUT THE KLC'S PRINCIPLES, MCPHERSON COLLEGE HAS:

Begun to increase enrollment and student retention by nontraditional means, blending the concepts of entrepreneurship into a liberal arts education. (Most of its peer schools have turned instead to adding athletic programs for recruitment.)

Energized faculty to incorporate entrepreneurial principles in the classroom and created an atmosphere that gives them room to take risks without fear.

Involved the entire campus community, rather than a narrow committee, to develop a strategic plan for growth over the next five years.

WHAT'S NEXT FOR MCPHERSON COLLEGE?

Continue to grow enrollment past the 1,000-student mark.

Build a $1 billion endowment.

Develop the residential college campus to meet the needs and expectations of the next generation of scholars.

KLC PRINCIPLE NO. 4

Your *purpose* must be clear.

IS YOUR PURPOSE CLEAR, OR ARE YOU JUST BUSY?

A legislator friend of mine once complained about all of her legislative meetings and official engagements. Running to committee meetings, reading bills, taking lunches with stakeholders and attending evening receptions kept her busy.

She said, "I never have time to do the things I really want to do." Her constituents elected her to help public schools and inner-city kids. I asked, "Why do you spend so much time going to committee meetings and receptions, the vast majority of which have no connection to schools or urban kids?"

She was silent and then said, "Do you expect me to skip my committee meetings and forgo the receptions with stakeholders?"

I said, "Yes, if that's what is needed to free up more time to spend on what you and your constituents really care about."

"I take my job seriously," she said. "I can't just not show up at things!"

"It sounds like you are busy but not productive," I replied. "Is your purpose to simply play the part of an elected official or to advance the things you care about?"

My guess is that we have all been in a spot like my friend. I'm certain that I have. We get too busy trying to play the part that we fail to get clear about purpose and hold to it.

QUESTIONS FOR REFLECTION:

> *Is your purpose clear? What would your life look like with Henry David Thoreau/Steve Jobs/Christina Long-like clarity of purpose?*

> *What would be different in your organization if its purpose was crystal clear?*

> *What competing purposes are you dealing with? Which one is winning?*

WHAT HAPPENS WHEN WE TRULY BELIEVE AND LIVE OUT
THE PRINCIPLE "YOUR PURPOSE MUST BE CLEAR"?
KLC ALUMS HAVE SOMETHING TO SAY ABOUT THAT.

"When the purpose is clear, it's a game changer."

PHYLLIS COLLINS
The Collins Network;
Kansas City, Missouri

"Clearly defined purposes will help all involved to stay focused. We call it 'plowing with purpose.'"

ADRION ROBERSON
DESTINY! Bible Fellowship Community
Church; Kansas City, Kansas

"When an organization truly believes and lives out the principle, 'your purpose must be clear,' all actions and strategies will align with the purpose. It will serve as the North Star in any given situation and will help build loyalty and engagement among those who stand behind that purpose."

NICOLE PFANNENSTIEL
Sunflower Electric Power Corp.; Hays, Kansas

Leadership Principle Nº 5

LEADERSHIP IS RARE, IT IS NOT THE NORM. IT'S THE EXCEPTION, NOT THE RULE.

Leadership is mobilizing others to make progress on daunting challenges. How often do you witness people being mobilized to make that kind of progress?

We believe leadership is rare because it is so risky. But why is it risky?

Leadership is risky for two reasons.

First, it's risky because you are disrupting the status quo, and the status quo — despite our complaints — usually works for most of us. And when you disrupt what is working for most people, they might not pat you on the back and say thank you. Instead, they might do whatever they can to resist. A common, and often subconscious, approach to resisting someone who is challenging the status quo is to discredit the individual.

Leadership
is *risky.*

"She just doesn't get us."

"He is clueless."

"She is only in it for herself."

More dramatic responses are to ostracize the individual, quit inviting them to meetings, even fire them. The risk of being discredited or removed keeps most of us from doing anything but exercising leadership. We'll do our part. We'll go through the motions. We'll keep completing the routine work. But rock the boat? Challenge the status quo? Raise the heat? Well, that's what exercising leadership looks like, and it just doesn't happen very often.

Second, it's risky because when you intervene, when you attempt to exercise leadership, there is a chance you could make things worse or be misunderstood. We rarely get points for good intentions. In the short run, it may feel safer to do nothing and just hope for change.

WHEN I COACHED MY SON'S BASEBALL TEAM AND MY DAUGHTER'S SOFTBALL TEAM, I ALWAYS TOLD KIDS THAT IF THEY WERE GOING TO STRIKE OUT THEY SHOULD STRIKE OUT SWINGING.

But what's available to you if you strike out looking? An excuse. You can always blame the umpire if you keep the bat on your shoulder. But you have no one to blame if you swing and miss. Swinging the bat can be risky.

In our organizations and communities, we lose the chance to blame others once we get involved, once we intervene. It's safer, especially when we aren't the one in charge, to just assume it's the job of the head person to lead, no matter what their title — CEO, pastor, executive director, senior manager or simply boss. That lets most of us off the hook for those risky behaviors of leadership.

LEADERSHIP ALWAYS INVOLVES RISK. YOU CAN'T ELIMINATE
THE RISK, BUT YOU CAN MITIGATE IT. HERE ARE THREE WAYS
TO LEARN ABOUT THE SKILLS AND TECHNIQUES TAUGHT AT THE
KANSAS LEADERSHIP CENTER TO MAKE LEADERSHIP LESS RISKY:

*Read "Your Leadership Edge: Lead Anytime, Anywhere"
by Ed O'Malley and Amanda Cebula for an overview of four
competencies taught at the KLC.*

*Visit www.yourleadershipedge.com and explore the online
home of our ideas.*

*Join us for our monthly virtual discussion called "On the Balcony."
(Search for "On the Balcony" at www.kansasleadershipcenter.org for
more information.)*

Leadership is risky. The risk can be mitigated. There are skills and techniques that make it more likely you can manage the risk, but you can't eliminate the risk. Risk is always a part of exercising leadership.

Few adaptive challenges in our communities feel riskier today than wading in on the topic of race relations, and specifically on the relationship between communities of color and law enforcement. It's an issue — a set of issues really — fraught with misunderstandings, implicit bias, history and personal experiences. It's hard to "go there" in a conversation. One misstep and you can be criticized as being anti-law enforcement or racist. So intervening in any way is risky. And perhaps that risk is exactly why we aren't making the progress our society so desperately needs on these issues.

This chapter tells two stories of KLC alums who waded into that issue — despite the risks — and utilized their leadership skills to make progress.

IN THE SUMMER OF 2014, THE NATION'S ATTENTION WAS RIVETED ON FERGUSON, MISSOURI, A ST. LOUIS SUBURB. MICHAEL BROWN, AN 18-YEAR-OLD AFRICAN-AMERICAN ACCUSED OF THEFT FROM A CONVENIENCE STORE, WAS SHOT AND KILLED BY DARREN WILSON, A WHITE POLICE OFFICER, IN THE MIDDLE OF A STREET ON A SATURDAY AFTERNOON.

It would be months before due process ran its course — with Wilson neither indicted by a local grand jury nor charged with a federal civil-rights violation — but the shooting loosened a cascade of pent-up emotions and tension in Ferguson, a city of about 20,000. Peaceful protesters in the majority-black city chanted, "Hands up, don't shoot." But there was looting and other violence, and the governor established a curfew and turned over law enforcement operations to the Missouri Highway Patrol, which showed up with military-style vehicles.

Some 400 miles away, leaders in Wichita's African-American community began mobilizing. They didn't want what had happened in Ferguson to happen in their community.

The Rev. Dr. Kevass Harding of Dellrose United Methodist Church, a predominantly African-American congregation, was on an annual guys' golfing trip when he saw news about the civil unrest in Ferguson: "You saw the frustration and anger, and I said, 'Man, that can happen in any city.'"

Kevass had a special vantage point for considering the tension between the law enforcement and minority communities: He is an African-American pastor who was once a Wichita police officer.

"There's great cops, and I felt like I was one of them, but there's instances where police brutality really exists," Kevass said.

He resolved to do something pre-emptive — to help turn down the heat between police and minority groups in Wichita before any crisis arose.

"You're not going to please everybody. You need to be able to understand that internally, or it can really mess you up because most people want to be liked."

REV. DR. KEVASS HARDING
Lead Pastor, Dellrose United Methodist Church

"I'll be an agitator if I have to be, but I'd rather be a collaborator," Kevass said.

One of his first calls was to another African-American church leader, the Rev. Junius Dotson, senior pastor at St. Mark United Methodist Church.

Framed on Junius' desk were the results of a personality test. "Thinker" got the highest bar, but the results also described him as an imaginer, a promoter and a rebel.

Junius was in. Kevass and Junius began planning a community forum, but they wanted results, not just another hall filled with people venting.

"The goal was not just to have a meeting where nothing would happen," Junius said. "We felt that this issue belonged to the whole city."

They moved quickly, bringing together the mayor, city manager, a City Council member, the interim police chief, the sheriff, community organizers and several others.

Junius wanted viable action items.

"How do we bring together people?" he asked. "It's not just a black issue."

"The goal was not just to have a meeting where nothing would happen. We felt that this issue belonged to the whole city."

REV. JUNIUS DOTSON
Senior Pastor, St. Mark United Methodist Church

The racial tensions across the nation added a sense of urgency. They decided on a forum, drew from their constituencies, created flyers and took to social media.

"We don't want what happened in Ferguson to happen here," was repeated again and again.

Thus, a hashtag was born: #NoFergusonHere, and on Aug. 28, 2014 — a scant two and a half weeks after Michael Brown's death — more than 600 Wichitans showed up for a community forum on police relations.

"It was one of the most beautiful meetings culturally," Kevass said, reflecting on the diverse crowd.

Kevass and Junius served as moderators. As people began discussing their concerns with their relationship with police officers, the organizers were careful to record responses.

At the end of that August evening, Kevass, Junius, and fellow forum organizers, were riding high. They had expected some anger, but they were optimistic about the ideas that emerged.

"Wichita is going to be one of those cities that's going to be an example," thought Junius.

When the organizers met again, they categorized the responses from the #NoFergusonHere forum and came up with four priorities:

> *Buy body cameras for the police force and require all officers to wear them.*
>
> *Implement crisis-intervention training for all officers.*
>
> *Create an independent review board for officer-involved shootings and allegations of misconduct.*
>
> *Increase the culture of community policing, which promotes trusting partnerships with residents, who then can be proactive when it comes to public safety and reducing crime.*

The organizers widely proclaimed this action plan, buckled down to make progress on all the points and announced a follow-up meeting. They were checking all the boxes, they thought, for achieving civic progress.

And that progress was happening at lightning speed: The city of Wichita committed to implementing body cameras for every patrol officer, locating funding sources and developing policies to regulate their use. When that happened — with a goal of full implementation by Dec. 31, 2015 — Wichita would be one of the first cities of its size to require all its officers to wear body cameras.

That's why Kevass and Junius were stunned by what happened at the second meeting, in December 2014, when about 200 people showed up at the city convention center.

The agenda consisted of a progress report and then small-group discussions. But those in attendance didn't want to talk in small groups. They wanted to vent to the whole group.

Junius and Kevass again served as moderators. They were caught off-guard by all the anger and frustration.

Kevass put it bluntly: "I felt attacked. We'd done all this work. We were very transparent."

Kevass and Junius managed their emotions as best they could and carried on with the meeting.

"Police work helped me understand: Don't take stuff personal," Kevass said. "You're not going to please everybody. You need to be able to understand that internally, or it can really mess you up because most people want to be liked."

It turned out to be a matter of managing expectations. Junius and Kevass had not anticipated that the intensity of the attendees' emotions would still be as high. They did their best to steer the group back to the agenda and the small-group discussions. At the end of the evening, they felt good about their progress. They felt the open dialogue and the concrete action items would help Wichita avoid what had erupted in Ferguson.

BY LIVING OUT THE KLC'S PRINCIPLES, JUNIUS AND KEVASS HAVE:

Successfully advocated for body cameras for all Wichita patrol officers.	Increased the culture of community policing.	Avoided the riot of emotion that erupted in Ferguson, Missouri.

Today, Junius and Kevass view their #NoFergusonHere efforts as a success. They and their fellow organizers have taken the four priorities identified in the initial meeting and have gone to work on all of them, in some cases making significant progress. Kevass was involved in Wichita's search for a new police chief, and the city implemented body cameras for all patrol officers. Both activists believe the implementation of body cameras would not have been accomplished so quickly without the catalyzing events of Ferguson and the momentum created by the #NoFergusonHere movement.

Kevass is also pleased with the increased culture of community policing. As for the other items on the list, he's satisfied with the progress on crisis-intervention training but does not think he has seen much action on the independent review of officer-involved shootings.

The status of the relationship between police and members of Wichita's African-American community is harder to quantify.

Junius has since left the state to take on a role with the United Methodist denomination's Discipleship Ministries. Kevass remains in Wichita, determined to keep plugging away at improving relationships with law enforcement officers and renewing focus on community policing.

"We still have a lot of 'that's not my problem' when it should be 'this is all of our problem,'" Kevass said.

WHAT'S NEXT FOR JUNIUS AND KEVASS?

Continue to advocate for the priorities that were identified as a result of the two community meetings.

Kevass wants to keep pushing for improvements in community policing and crisis-intervention training.

TRUE TO THE ADAPTIVE NATURE OF THE ISSUE, THE #NOFERGUSONHERE MOVEMENT DIDN'T SOLVE EVERYTHING.

It may have avoided a confrontation and planted seeds for the future, demonstrating the type of leadership — convening, engaging and still provocative — needed for progress. It would have been easier for Junius and Kevass, both KLC alums, to do nothing. They put themselves in a position to accept a lot of criticism — especially at the second meeting where the heat was elevated and much of it was channeled at them. They held steady, accepted the risk and kept trying.

BRANDON JOHNSON LEARNED FIRSTHAND THAT FINDING COMMON GROUND SOMETIMES MEANS ACCEPTING RISK.

The KLC alumnus embraced the leadership principle of "it's risky" when he and others agreed to forgo a planned protest in the summer of 2016 in favor of the First Steps Community Cookout, an event proposed by Wichita Police Chief Gordon Ramsay to dial back community tensions. The event came days after Black Lives Matter supporters and protesters had marched in Wichita amid national turmoil over the shootings of black civilians and police officers.

"We all knew what the fallout to us would be if we accepted it," Brandon said. "That's something that no one ever wants to talk about."

WHILE MANY KLC PARTICIPANTS ENGAGE WITH THE CENTER TO HELP MAKE PROGRESS ON ORGANIZATIONAL CHALLENGES, 53 PERCENT OF KLC ALUMNI SEE THEMSELVES AS PERSONALLY AND ACTIVELY INVOLVED IN EFFORTS TO ADDRESS KEY COMMUNITY CHALLENGES IN KANSAS — AND MANY OF THOSE COMMUNITY CHALLENGES ARE FRAUGHT WITH RISK.

But he wouldn't change a thing.

There was immediate national media attention, much of it focusing on the two sides finding common ground and easing tension. While Ramsay subsequently received an invitation to the White House, there was fallout for Brandon and local activists A.J. Bohannon and Djuan Wash. The event was criticized by Black Lives Matter, and the men were labeled as traitors by some for sitting at the table with the police.

BRANDON JOHNSON
Community Activist and Founder,
Community Operations Recovery Empowerment

What many don't know, Brandon said, is that they accepted the risk after the chief also agreed to shoulder some himself. Ramsay made several verbal commitments, ranging from agreeing to have more crisis-intervention training for officers, implementing some police tactics that can save lives and adding more officers to build on the concept of community policing. He also agreed not to oppose the creation of a citizen review board or the concept of a special prosecutor to investigate police-related shootings.

"The story of what actually happened there was never told," Brandon said.

The chief also agreed to answer questions for 90 minutes at the cookout. It was a turning point for organizers, according to Brandon.

"So for 90 minutes he stood out in front of the community, which was the real reason behind the barbecue — to get him out there and also build this trust," Brandon said. "It got him out there in front of a community that always feels targeted and overlooked and had him answer directly to them."

The chief kept his word and stood before the public without notes.

"I'm always giving him the utmost respect for doing that, because no other chief has," Brandon said. "It was tough, but he did it. He was truthful and said as much as he possibly could."

Brandon doesn't believe that message was lost on the hundreds who attended that day, even if it was lost in some media reports. There were lines for the food, bounce houses and other attractions. But there was an equally long line, he said, to approach the microphone and ask the chief a question.

"That was what we wanted," he said.

The risks both sides took that day have opened up the lines of communication in a way that hasn't happened in recent years, Brandon said.

GORDON RAMSAY
Chief of Police, Wichita

"Ramsay has been the most open, transparent and willing chief that we've had," he said.

It has rebuilt trust. That's crucial, given that many of the commitments the chief offered will take time to come to fruition. State mandates have made it difficult to create a special prosecutor, and hiring dozens of new officers will take time. Yet Brandon is hardly discouraged. He thinks the department is open to new ideas.

"To me, since the barbecue, I have seen a much more friendly and open department," he said. "You don't always get the answer you want to hear, but at least you actually get an answer."

There have been several small, but significant, steps to strengthen community relationships including a recent workshop aimed at demystifying "the gang file." The topic has long frustrated residents, who wanted to know how people were being added to and deleted from the list. Its mysterious nature made it easy for those outside the department to dress it up with sinister intentions.

A police lieutenant wanted the public to know more, Brandon said.

"So we held a workshop. He came out and he explained everything. He brought out the beat officer for the area," Brandon said. "They've been open

BY LIVING OUT THE KLC'S PRINCIPLES,
BRANDON HAS:

Taken the first steps toward rebuilding trust between the police chief and communities of color.

Created the groundwork for meaningful community input on the gang file, a citizen's review board, new police tactics, crisis intervention training and a special prosecutor to investigate police-related shootings.

about doing that, and they said that they'll do that anytime we want to. They really want to build those relationships."

Other changes may never be noticed by casual observers. There may not be headlines when police peacefully end violent standoffs or employ other new tactics that save lives, but Brandon is hopeful that a new era has begun.

"Things are changing," he said. "We're moving in the right direction."

WHAT'S NEXT FOR BRANDON?

Hold government officials, including the police chief, accountable for following through on their commitments. Provide government officials with the support necessary to move forward.

Brandon will also hold himself accountable when it comes to unifying the community. Elected to serve on the Wichita City Council in 2017, he has pledged to continue efforts to unify the community, because consistency is essential and momentum cannot be lost.

As soon as the idea for the cookout surfaced, Brandon experienced pushback from peers and colleagues. There was risk in going forward for him and others.

Adaptive challenges are filled with risks. When you are leading others in adaptive work, you are helping them literally adapt. They are changing, letting go of their current way of working and taking on new approaches. Risk is inherent. Also, when we do something new, we might not do it well, and that brings additional risk.

It's often easier to continue down a current path, rather than attempt something new.

Kevass, Junius and Brandon each made a decision to attempt something new. Decisions have real consequences and exercising leadership requires you to make myriad decisions, each one with the potential to alienate some group or faction connected to your issue.

By deciding to accept the offer of a cookout, Brandon alienated members of the African-American community who didn't want any collaboration with the police. The courage to make decisions, even when you don't have all the information you would prefer, is part of leadership. And making decisions on tough issues feels risky and consequential.

IN 2014, I CHEERFULLY WALKED INTO THE COURTHOUSE TO PERFORM MY CIVIC DUTY. I WOULDN'T HAVE BELIEVED YOU IF YOU TOLD ME THE NEXT NINE DAYS WOULD BE SEARED INTO MY MEMORY.

I dreamed about the case each night of the trial. A murder trial has a way of sticking with you even outside the courtroom.

I didn't sleep well the night before we delivered the verdict, either. The weight of the decision was heavy.

I assume the accused didn't sleep well, either. Or his family and friends or the other members of the jury.

People talk about jury service in terms of civic duty and responsibility. Ever since that trial, I've talked about it as tough decision-making, too.

Making decisions may be an undervalued art in this interesting world of leadership development in which I live. We help people diagnose a situation, engage others, speak from the heart, manage emotions, challenge the norms, hold to purpose and so on. But all of that is weak if someone struggles to decide yes or no, now or later, guilty or not guilty.

It was a complicated case. I found myself longing for a simple case of bad guy hurts good guy. This was a case full of bad guys hurting one another. It wasn't cut and dried.

Isn't life, and therefore leadership, like that too? Everything is a shade of gray. Truth is a fantasy. Leadership must be about navigating the many truths out there and finding a way to help people move forward. The jury heard lots of versions of the truth. I believe that someone who honestly believed it to be the truth told each version. It was up to us to sit in judgment.

We had to decide guilt or innocence. We were not advisers. We were not consultants. We had to make the decision — each of us personally and the group collectively.

The moment before I shared my opinion with my fellow jurors felt familiar. It was as if I were back in the Kansas House of Representatives, about to vote on a controversial matter, looking at the red and green buttons on my desk. Red meant no, green meant yes. Green or red. Yes or no.

There comes a time in most situations where, if you intend to lead, you must make decisions. You might not have all the facts. You rarely will be fully comfortable. You usually can't be certain that you are 100 percent right and zero percent wrong. Decisions on tough matters are usually more like 70-30 or 60-40.

A few of the jurors were struggling under the pressure of it all. They were frozen. Unable to agree with a clear majority, but also unable to present a clear line of logic to suggest that the majority needed to change its mind. This was heavy work, and they were entitled to take as much time as they needed.

My sense was that these few jurors were struggling with the same thing that haunts so many people in so many situations that require leadership — coming to grips with the reality of their decisions and the consequences for all involved. Eventually they agreed with the rest of the jurors on a guilty verdict. But my sense was that they would have rather avoided making a decision.

Progress on so many adaptive challenges remains elusive and only comes when people decide to act experimentally. When they decide to try something, learn from that experiment and then decide to try something else again, and again and again.

> *In Kansas we are building the capacity of people to act, to make decisions on behalf of more progress on the things that matter most to their organizations and communities. They know there are risks involved and it's inspiring seeing Kansans like Brandon, Kevass, Junius, Gordon and so many more decide to act despite the risks.*

KLC PRINCIPLE NO. 5

Leadership is *risky.*

A colleague recently sent an image around the office that read: *If you want to make everyone happy, don't be a leader — sell ice cream.* That just about sums up this chapter.

There is a reason why progress on adaptive challenges is elusive. People would rather not change. Leadership on adaptive challenges means you are unabashedly mobilizing people and systems to change. When you do that, you will get pushback.

The uncomfortable corollary is that if you are not getting pushback, you probably aren't exercising leadership. However, just because you are getting pushback doesn't mean you are leading. Your ideas might be poor, your skills and tactics could be off, etc. But make no mistake, if you are truly exercising leadership on an adaptive challenge, you will experience pushback, at least at the beginning.

Leadership is extremely rare, and it's rare because it is so risky.

QUESTIONS FOR REFLECTION:

>   *What would happen if those in your organization
>   or community understood the risks associated with leading?*

>   *What would be possible if you could mitigate the risks associated
>   with leading? (Our book "Your Leadership Edge" and KLC
>   programs help people do this.)*

>   *What do you care enough about in your organization or
>   community that you are willing to take on the risks that
>   come with exercising leadership?*

WHAT HAPPENS WHEN WE TRULY BELIEVE AND LIVE OUT
THE PRINCIPLE "LEADERSHIP IS RISKY"?
KLC ALUMS HAVE SOMETHING TO SAY ABOUT THAT.

"People would begin
to act on their beliefs,
even if the consequences
could cause individual
sacrifice."

PETER COOK
Leadership Labette; Parsons, Kansas

"In many instances,
in order to proceed
or make progress, you
must go out on a limb
or do things that are not
comfortable. I truly believe
that we must do what is
right and not necessarily
what is comfortable."

BECKY WOLFE
*Andover Area Chamber of Commerce;
Andover, Kansas*

"If we truly take risks, we will do some things that seem
crazy at first but then become the norm. Or they end
up becoming a stupid idea that we joke about. Either
way, we did something that we weren't sure would
work to help us learn and move forward faster."

THOMAS STANLEY
Kansas Leadership Center; Wichita, Kansas

CONCLUSION

Scale Matters

I recently visited with a retired Marine about how the Marine Corps instills leadership qualities throughout its ranks. The discussion reminded me of the hours I spent as a kid reading through Dad's "Guidebook for Marines." I still have it. It can teach you anything: how to march, how to dress appropriately for formal events, how to fire a bazooka. It also is filled with implicit and explicit leadership lessons.

While there are clear lines of hierarchy and authority in the Marine Corps, it is an organization that inherently understands that leadership is an activity, not a position, and that leadership needs to be cultivated on a large scale throughout the organization.

I believe most leadership development efforts get wrong what the Marine Corps gets right. Adaptive challenges cannot be solved by authority alone.

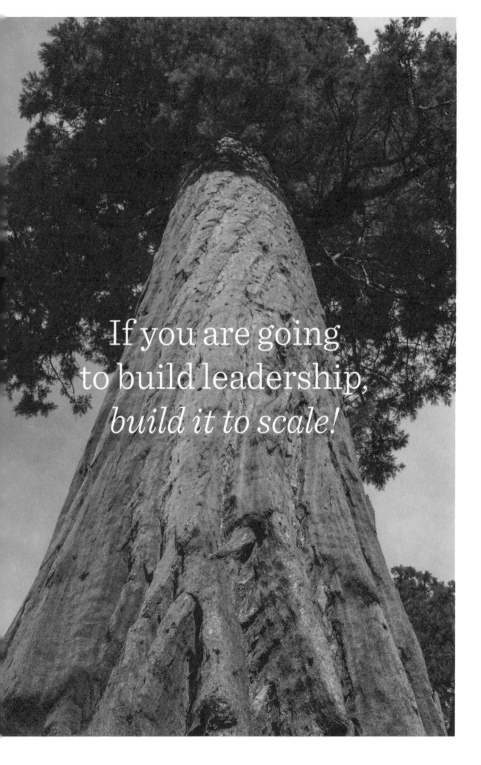

If you are going
to build leadership,
build it to scale!

Large organizational, community or societal adaptive challenges cannot be solved with just a few people exercising tremendous leadership. Progress is made when large numbers of people begin engaging and leading in ways consistent with adaptive work.

PROGRESS IS MADE WHEN LARGE NUMBERS OF PEOPLE BEGIN ACTING EXPERIMENTALLY, WORKING ACROSS FACTIONS, ENGAGING UNUSUAL VOICES, RAISING THE HEAT AND CHOOSING AMONG COMPETING VALUES.

Why? Because when enough people throughout a system begin exuding behaviors consistent with adaptive work, the culture itself begins to take on those qualities. And once that happens, real progress can be made.

One person in a company who is able to step back, get up on the balcony and discern what's adaptive and what's technical is useful. But a large percentage of people in the same company able to exercise that same skill creates a culture that naturally, over time, is able to separate the adaptive from the technical, allowing the company to thrive.

When it comes to leadership development, scale matters.

The Kansas Leadership Center is trying to transform the civic culture of Kansas so it becomes a culture that solves problems and seizes opportunities faster, more effectively and more efficiently. We work with individuals, but our aim is to change the culture. Doing so requires us to work with enough individuals throughout the state so that cultural change, over time, becomes possible.

Most leadership development efforts work with a relatively small group. A nonprofit with 400 employees occasionally sends one or two people to leadership training. A company with thousands of employees engages only a very small number of those employees in leadership training.

Our approach is vastly different, and we are glad our approach is taking hold in other places across our state and beyond.

Maybe you are in the leadership development business. Maybe you finance leadership programs or teach them. If so, what's the scale of your effort? Are you working to imbed leadership throughout your organization or community? Or are you really working just to help a handful of people learn leadership? The former is a pathway to progress on adaptive challenges. The latter can be helpful to individuals, but rarely changes a culture.

We are transforming the civic culture of Kansas.

Those trying to do good things in the world often long for cultural change. They envision a culture of innovation and initiative within a company. They crave a culture of inclusion and empowerment in a community. They desire a culture of evangelism in a faith community. And cultural change only happens after enough people take up the work and engage differently.

Many of us in the leadership development world want a culture of leadership in our communities and organizations, a culture that acts adaptively, a culture that energizes others and blazes new trails.

Creating a culture of leadership will require us to work on a scale atypical for most leadership development efforts.

79% OF ALUMNI REPORT TEACHING THE KLC IDEAS TO OTHERS OR USING THEM IN THEIR COACHING OF PEERS OR COLLEAGUES.

Here are three stories of organizations doing just that.

SUNFLOWER ELECTRIC POWER CORPORATION

Two Sunflower Electric managers — in two different communities — independently participated in fledgling Kansas Leadership Center programs. After discovering their joint connection to the center and the empowering aspects of its curriculum, the two women persuaded senior leaders to not only extend training opportunities to employees but also to embed KLC principles into a reimagined corporate culture.

Long before they became part of the executive team themselves, Clare Gustin, vice president of member services and external affairs, and Jana Horsfall, vice president of corporate services, diagnosed Sunflower's situation, including unprecedented industry changes and an aging workforce. They understood that technical solutions previously relied upon would no longer suffice and believed an in-house leadership program could help the company successfully navigate through business transitions.

Their initial training focus was on managers, but "two days in on a six-day training program, the participants said more employees needed to have access to the material, so we broadened it to include supervisors and ultimately every employee," Clare said.

Carol Haberman, manager of organizational development, and Nikki Pfannenstiel, manager of member services, currently facilitate Sunflower's fall leadership program for new employees each year.

CAROL HABERMAN
Manager of Organizational Development, Sunflower Electric Power Corporation

The leadership program participants convene a month later for a second two-day session that focuses on competencies that have been incorporated into the company's culture statement. Every summer, all employees take a refresher course designed to keep the material top of mind and facilitate a dialogue about issues and opportunities.

"When you buy a car, you take it in for tune-ups and oil changes, and leadership training works the same way," Carol said. "Sometimes we share new information, but for the most part, we discuss communication and change and how we can improve our approaches using the familiar framework. Everything we discuss relates back to our culture statement and a focus on doing things better."

A continuous willingness to diagnose the company's situation shapes Sunflower's evolving strategy execution.

NIKKI PFANNENSTIEL
Manager of Member Services,
Sunflower Electric Power Corporation

"We try to uncover perceptions surrounding the stories people tell about our company and the work we do, from our cooperative members to our community partners, and then determine how we can intervene skillfully at the right time," Nikki said.

Sunflower's comprehensive leadership program is just one example of skillful intervention.

Succession planning is especially important to the company at this juncture in its history. Sunflower employs about 415 people, and Carol estimates that by December 2020, 25 percent of its vice presidents, 20 percent of its managers and 31 percent of its supervisors will be eligible for retirement.

To that end, Sunflower developed a model formulated with input from employees identifying competencies in alignment with KLC principles. Its culture statement says, "Sunflower values and expects all within the organization to behave in ways that consistently exhibit the following characteristics: technical competency; respect and dignity; accountability; integrity; trustworthiness; and servant leadership."

Beyond the foundational qualities that all employees must exhibit, individuals must demonstrate additional areas of strength and expertise to move through the four categories of increasing responsibility: technical and professional, supervisor, manager and executive.

CLARE GUSTIN
Vice President of Member Services and External Affairs, Sunflower Electric Power Corporation

"We can see the skills required for a position and then determine whether we can promote from within or need to recruit," Nikki said.

In December 2016, the company brought in a KLC facilitator to help the management team discuss adaptive versus technical approaches specific to the electric utility business. "We constantly have to re-evaluate and change as needed due to this changing environment. Helping our employees understand and adapt to that change is critical for our success," Carol said.

Looking at things through a new lens permeates every aspect of Sunflower's recruitment and retention initiatives — conducting career discussions in grade-school classrooms to encourage interest in utility positions, attending college career fairs, enhancing a college internship program, implementing flexible work schedules when feasible, piloting 360-degree assessments and incorporating language from the competency model to formulate interview questions and ongoing development programs.

BY LIVING OUT THE KLC'S PRINCIPLES,
SUNFLOWER ELECTRIC POWER CORP. HAS:

Identified the gap between where it is today and where it wants to be in the future.	Developed strategies to close the gap.	Equipped employees with a common understanding of leadership capacities needed to be successful in the organization.

WHAT'S NEXT FOR SUNFLOWER ELECTRIC?

Execute the strategies identified to get Sunflower Electric where it wants to be in the future and evolve the strategies as needed.

Continue to develop a diverse workforce equipped with competencies necessary to lead the utility through future organizational and industry challenges.

Clare, Carol and Nikki also facilitate leadership training sessions for area economic-development and strategic-planning groups and train-the-trainer programs to help other companies and communities striving to make progress on their own adaptive issues.

"Servant leadership and the concepts shared through KLC provide people the opportunity to not only practice these skills at work but also at home, at church or at volunteer organizations," Carol said.

For Jana, the most gratifying aspect of seeing Sunflower's leadership program come to fruition has been the "ageless characteristics of the competencies" she and Clare "learned so many years ago and couldn't wait to share. They blend innovation and common sense and have proven invaluable in helping us foster our successful culture and effective works."

"(The competencies) blend innovation and common sense and have proven invaluable in helping us foster our successful culture and effective works."

JANA HORSFALL
Vice President of Corporate Services,
Sunflower Electric Power Corporation

EMPORIA STATE UNIVERSITY

Emporia State University is determined to become "the adaptive university." It is incorporating adaptive leadership principles into the very fiber of its being.

In the spring of 2013, the then-president of Emporia State, Michael Shonrock, initiated a dialogue that has grown to a university-wide mission to infuse leadership principles throughout the campus. Rather than leadership training for a select few, Emporia State wants it for everyone, believing that's what's necessary to become a thriving university in the 21st century.

MICHAEL SHONROCK
Former President,
Emporia State University

In the beginning, the idea was to make general education courses more relevant by incorporating a leadership curriculum alongside the general curriculum. The idea has evolved into a powerful priority. A key has been a deep connection with the new Honors College.

Gary Wyatt directs the college and has been a part of a Kansas Leadership Center partnership with Emporia State since the beginning.

Any effort to build large-scale leadership must have an anchoring organization or institution. The KLC could be that for Kansas. The Honors College could be that for Emporia State. A training department could serve that function in an organization. But somehow, an anchoring organization with credibility and stature must champion the leadership training.

The Honors College gives the work of teaching adaptive leadership a permanent home on campus. Gary credits founding the Honors College as one of the two most important steps the university has taken to integrate adaptive leadership principles.

"Adaptive leadership is a critical component of the experience our honors students receive," Gary explained.

The mission of the Honors College is to prepare students to be "agents of change for the common good." All honors students receive civic leadership training in the form of a two-day immersive experience, and they find it embedded in honors courses.

The mission to advance adaptive leadership does not exist solely in the Honors College. Adaptive leadership is a part of the university's 2015-2025 strategic plan and is reflected in a university mission statement: "Preparing students for lifelong learning, rewarding careers and adaptive leadership." This bedrock commitment has survived despite turnover in key roles. After Michael took another job, the project was embraced by the new administration. Current President Allison D. Garrett is equally committed to advancing adaptive leadership.

Nathan Woolard, who headed the Department of Leadership Studies, also left for another job. But because the task of incorporating adaptive leadership hadn't been left to a single department or department head, the program continues to flourish.

"Adaptive leadership is a critical component of the experience our honors students receive."

GARY WYATT
Associate Provost and Director of the Honors College, Emporia State University

Incorporating leadership into strategic goals and the university mission has helped rally the university around a collective purpose. Its close relationship with the KLC has continued as well. The presidential cabinet receives refresher courses on KLC competencies, and leadership training is a regular part of campus life.

For cultural change to occur at Emporia State, in the state of Kansas or in your organization, the drive for the change can't come from one individual or department. If the drive comes from diverse and disparate individuals and groups, change can take hold and withstand individuals moving in and out of the picture. If we want a culture of leadership, we have to work on a scale large enough that it fosters this kind of ownership.

Including adaptive leadership in strategic goals and mission statements is an important symbolic step that affirms executive intentions, but Emporia State also acted in accord with these words, providing the resources and support to make them a reality.

In the early stages of the KLC experiment, Gary thought success or failure would be based on the faculty's acceptance of adaptive leadership concepts. Even now, despite widespread enthusiasm for adaptive leadership, it's not uncommon for some faculty members to think that adaptive leadership is merely the latest educational fad, doomed to abandonment once excitement has faded.

"We've had to assure the faculty we're committed," Gary said. This commitment is visible in a KLC faculty-in-residence program that continually expands the university's capacity to teach and demonstrate adaptive leadership.

Each semester, selected faculty members receive KLC training, embed adaptive leadership principles in their curriculum and regularly offer training to other faculty and staff.

BY LIVING OUT THE KLC'S PRINCIPLES, EMPORIA STATE UNIVERSITY HAS:

Created a living
model for leadership.

Transformed
university life.

WHAT'S NEXT FOR EMPORIA STATE UNIVERSITY?

Consider how to incorporate leadership principles into other corners of campus, such as the residence hall environment and campus environment for residents.

Develop an expanding fellowship of KLC Faculty in Residence.

"It's part of a strategic plan to increase the number of courses with adaptive leadership embedded in them," Gary said.

But Emporia State wants to do more than teach adaptive leadership. The university wants to cultivate students and faculty who are dedicated to taking action for the common good, and understanding and using the tools of adaptive leadership to make a real difference in their communities.

"Adaptive leadership is becoming a very important part of this entire university," Gary observed.

At Emporia State, the goal is not just to teach adaptive leadership but to be the adaptive university. If it had an official leadership motto, it might be "more leadership for all."

PROJECT 17

Most of us can conjure up a mental picture of the audience at an economic-development discussion, like the one held a few years ago in Ottawa, Kansas, where speaker after speaker shared opinions on what it would take to bolster the fortunes of the cities and counties of southeast Kansas. Amid that collection of experts was a woman who, after listening attentively, offered some thoughtful and personal assistance. "I am a widower," she said. "I'm in my 80s. I don't have much I can give back. But I can talk and sit and be a friend to somebody. I can help." With that, she joined forces with more than 1,900 Kansans in an innovative regional program called Project 17.

Formed in 2011, Project 17 was created specifically to find solutions to issues in 17 economically hard-hit Kansas counties, according to the group's executive director, Heather Morgan.

"The region is a pocket of generational poverty," Heather said. "Entire families here have never known anything but poverty. Even if they do have jobs, the pay tends to be low. They're the working poor."

Heather said her group approaches economic development "in a cross-sector fashion that involves jobs, education, health and grassroots leadership.

"We firmly believe that you can't have economic development without a strong workforce. And you can't have a strong workforce with people who aren't healthy. And you can't move forward to a good business climate without leadership."

JEFF TUCKER
Executive Director,
Advanced Manufacturing Institute

Originally, Heather said, legislators "were going to throw money at the project and hope good things happened." But quickly it became clear that Project 17 could only succeed by acting on directions from the very people who were living daily with the effects of a failing economy.

"We had to move past the thinking that if only an expert would tell us what to do, everything would be solved. That's not going to happen."

HEATHER MORGAN
Executive Director, Project 17

"Project 17 is a grassroots-up as opposed to a top-level-down initiative," said Jeff Tucker, whose Advanced Manufacturing Institute at Kansas State University became an early project partner. "Rather than coming in and saying, 'These are the things that we're going to do,' we've tried to identify the energy and the passion of people, and then bring in other outside resources to accelerate those efforts."

With training from the KLC, Project 17 volunteers learned to take on new, unimagined responsibilities. "One of the key competencies of KLC is that anyone can lead, anytime, anywhere," Heather said. "We had to move past the thinking that if only an expert would tell us what to do, everything would be solved. That's not going to happen."

Instead, the volunteers grew less dependent on traditional leaders and began to see themselves as the experts. Heather said her group practices adaptive problem solving. "People learned there's no one way to solve a problem — and there's likely no one solution that will solve everything. It's a matter of 18 differently-thinking people working together around a common mission to make progress."

Project 17 also works to create economic pride and loyalty in the region. "It's natural to look for 'something shiny' in economic development — the big national company coming in from somewhere else," she said. "But it's more important to support the businesses that are already here, who have ties that will keep them in our communities."

BY LIVING OUT THE KLC'S PRINCIPLES, HEATHER AND PROJECT 17 HAVE:

Shifted the region's focus from waiting for "experts" to solve problems to an approach that encourages people affected by the region's generational poverty to use their real-life expertise to offer solutions.

WHAT'S NEXT FOR PROJECT 17?

Although more than 1,900 volunteers have worked with Project 17 to create jobs, attract private investments, build technical infrastructure and expand educational opportunities, there are still population pockets that need to have a place at the Project 17 discussion table.

Continue building bridges between the area's schools and universities and regional businesses to make sure the counties' workforces are both well-versed in essential math and science skills and able to quickly adapt to new manufacturing and service opportunities

Less than 10 years and more than 1,900 volunteers after it began, the work of Project 17 shows results. Needs have been identified, skills learned and leadership put into practice.

More than 1,000 leaders have been trained, more than $25 million in private investments attained, nearly 200 businesses assisted, 670-plus jobs created and 430 jobs retained.

With help from Advanced Manufacturing, several Kansas colleges and the Kansas Fiber Network, the group worked to transition businesses from outdated dial-up connections to high-speed internet capabilities.

In 2014, Independence Community College created the first fabrication lab in the state featuring cutting-edge design and manufacturing tools that included 3-D technology. A second lab is planned for Chanute. Meanwhile, Pittsburg State University's Polymer Chemistry Initiative offers training and degrees in the promising polymer chemistry field.

"Training from the Kansas Leadership Center teaches people how to transform their communities," said Elaine Johannes, an associate professor in K-State's School of Family Studies and Human Services. "That's what's happening here. They're creating common goals and following those words with actions, getting it done. People's lives are being changed."

ELAINE JOHANNES
Associate Professor, Kansas State University School of Family Studies and Human Services

Heather added, "We're taking ownership and saying, 'I want to help my neighbor. I want my community to be a better place. I want this place to be good for my kids and my grandkids and the next generation. I want my kids to come back to someplace they can be proud of.'"

The city manager of Pittsburg, Daron Hall, sees a simple strength in the program. "I think it's a roadmap to success," he said. "Project 17 should be a model for the rest of the state. Look beyond your borders, not only for solutions but to lend a hand."

"It's not as hard as you'd think to make a difference if you just pay attention and try. We are not alone. We're at our best when we're helping others."

DARON HALL
City Manager, Pittsburg

I OFTEN DESCRIBE THE KANSAS LEADERSHIP CENTER
AS "LARGE-SCALE LEADERSHIP DEVELOPMENT." THAT'S
WHAT WE'VE BEEN DOING FOR A DECADE AND WILL
CONTINUE TO DO. HERE'S OUR LATEST EXAMPLE
OF LARGE-SCALE THINKING:

Wyandotte County consistently ranks as one of the unhealthiest counties in Kansas. It's one of the most economically depressed, too, especially the urban core of Kansas City, Kansas. Some of the historic neighborhoods, which were once home to doctors and attorneys, are now home to abandoned houses. It's hard to find fresh produce in the urban core. I could go on.

Yet there is a spirit of resolve and a passion among the people who live there to improve the community and help people thrive.

The Kansas Leadership Center's board of directors recently adopted a goal of training 500 participants each year from Kansas City, Kansas. There is great leadership in Kansas City, but we can all do better. Even the best leaders need time to reflect and hone their skills. And those who have never taken the initiative to lead can learn to do so.

We believe there are hundreds of people in that community who are interested and excited to improve their leadership. But in a recent conversation with a prominent organization in the greater Kansas City area, I was disheartened when I heard, "Ed, I don't think you'll find 500 leaders there."

I get this person's point. If we think about leadership in traditional ways — as the people with key roles and lots of authority — there might not be 500 people a year to engage in training. That's how most people think about leadership training: It's for those in key positions or those who will soon be in key positions.

As you know by now, we at the KLC think quite differently. We think leadership is an activity, not a position. That it can be done by anyone, anytime, anywhere. Are there 500 people in Kansas City, Kansas, interested in leading to improve their community? By all means yes!

If we imagine leadership in this way — disconnected from authority and as an activity — it opens up new ways of thinking. It's not enough to just have a few key people leading in a community; we need vast numbers of people exercising leadership. Rather than an exclusive leadership program for the select few, now we could (and must if we want progress on deep, daunting, adaptive work) think about leadership development on a scale large enough to create a culture of leadership.

The adaptive challenges facing our organizations and communities can be solved if we build a culture of leadership. A culture of leadership can transform your organization. A culture of leadership can transform our state.

In the introduction I compared leadership to baseball. Just like baseball players strive to improve their batting average, I mentioned that we are trying to raise the "leadership average" of Kansans. As we do, more progress will be made on tough issues, such as the progress described in the stories included in this book. We work with more Kansans each year, getting ever closer to a tipping point. There will come a time when Kansas will naturally be a place that lives out these principles.

The Sunflower State?

The Wheat State?

In time, you'll think of Kansas as The Leadership State.

Onward!

QUESTIONS FOR REFLECTION:

What is the scale of your leadership development efforts?

What would it look like to build the leadership capacity of enough people in your organization or community to actually create a culture of leadership?

How long would it take to create a culture of leadership in your organization? What would you need to do to sustain your efforts over that time?

What
impact
have the
KLC principles
had on
organizations
across
the state?

"Since we have connected with KLC and embraced the competencies as a part of our curriculum, I have noticed that our classes are not only stronger but more connected with each other. They stay together as a group longer than those before them. I credit having to be more vulnerable, to speak from the heart and to work out issues from a 'below the neck' perspective for having a long-lasting impact on our program."

SUE HACK
Leadership Lawrence,
The Chamber of Lawrence;
Lawrence, Kansas

"KLC is important because its leadership principles and the underlying competencies capture the essence of leadership. KLC is particularly talented and uniquely skilled at teaching these important concepts which empower all those who are exposed/trained in the competencies to make progress on important issues and bring about change in their respective environments."

SUSAN KANG
KU Endowment;
Lawrence, Kansas

"KLC listened to Kansans and developed a leadership strategy based on a solid foundation to create stronger, healthier and more confident leaders."

CAROLYN KENNETT
Parsons, Kansas

"KLC keeps the research, study, demonstration and impact of 'leadership' in the collective consciousness of Kansans and all those who participate in its programs."

PHYLLIS COLLINS
The Collins Network;
Kansas City, Missouri

"KLC brings the opportunity for people to take a risk and to look at exercising leadership with pertinent competencies and principles. It is also a belief system … KLC has proven to me to be a valuable resource and training tool and I trust in the philosophy."

BECKY WOLFE
Andover Area Chamber of Commerce; Andover, Kansas

"KLC nurtures and encourages our organizations, communities and individuals to exercise leadership on the really tough issues, especially when the answer is not clear. Through the common understanding of the leadership principles, KLC is creating a concentration of leaders who, when rallied around a common purpose, can really make a difference."

NIKKI PFANNENSTIEL
Sunflower Electric Power Corp.;
Hays, Kansas

"As the person responsible for the entire organization, KLC ideas have helped me to empower others to be creative in the application of their tasks. My managers have turned out to be leaders, and as a consequence, my company has grown substantially during the past five years."

PETER COOK
Leadership Labette;
Parsons, KS

"KLC is one of the few organizations that is wild with optimism yet proposes a very conservative approach to changing human behavior."

TIM STEFFENSMEIER
Kansas State University; Manhattan, Kansas

"KLC is a gathering place (an actual address, a virtual space, an idea) for people who want to make things better, who are dissatisfied with the status quo, and who are willing to change their own behavior — or their own mindset — in order to make the world, the organization, the community or the company better for themselves and others."

JULIA FABRIS MCBRIDE
Kansas Leadership Center;
Wichita, Kansas

"KLC is important because … 'good enough' isn't enough anymore. Because mediocrity can't continue to be the victor. Because our challenges aren't getting smaller or going away just because we want them to."

RACQUEL THIESEN
KLC contractor;
Newton, Kansas

"KLC forces the individual to truly think outside of the box and inside the heart. … #transformational."

ADRION ROBERSON
DESTINY! Bible Fellowship Community Church;
Kansas City, Kansas

"So many people waste time and money on the quick fixes to the daunting challenges that exist. KLC truly helps push people to take on adaptive challenges using adaptive approaches."

THOMAS STANLEY
Kansas Leadership Center;
Wichita, Kansas

"At no other recent time in history has politics been more divisive, have working families struggled so much and our future been so uncertain. Effective leadership is critical to all these and other challenges."

LALO MUNOZ
El Centro of Topeka;
Topeka, Kansas

"KLC has been absolutely key in the transformation of our community-based leadership program from a good program about our communities to a program that balances that important piece with leadership skills that allow for personal, professional and community growth!"

MARY JANE CHAPMAN
Facilitator for Leadership Mitchell County;
Beloit, Kansas

Acknowledgments

I am thankful to work closely with the managing editor of The Journal, Chris Green, whose creativity, hard work and smarts have cultivated The Journal and his team into a special and powerful force in our state. This book would not have been possible without the foundation created by Chris.

I am grateful for a team of writers, many of whom regularly write for The Journal, who helped bring this book to life. The stories included in the book were drafted by these writers, who did a wonderful job bringing out the heart of the KLC ideas. The following writers helped with this book:

CHRIS
GREEN

ANNE
DEWVALL

ERIN
O'DONNELL

JOE
STUMPE

LAURA
RODDY

DAWN
NOVASCONE

BOB
HAMRICK

MARK
MCCORMICK

KIM
GRONNIGER

AMY
GEISZLER-JONES

PATSY
TERRELL

ACKNOWLEDGMENTS CONT.

Dozens of KLC alumni are featured or quoted in this book. I appreciate their willingness to share their stories and to exercise leadership for the common good.

The idea for this book came from Steve Coen, president and CEO of the Kansas Health Foundation. A champion of the KLC, Steve has lived out the principles in this book over and over as he built support for KLC within the foundation.

I am grateful to Marty Linsky and Ron Heifetz for enriching our understanding of leadership on adaptive challenges and to David Chrislip for nurturing KLC's orientation to the common good. Marty never stops pushing and inspiring me. His mentorship and friendship guided my discovery of many of the ideas in this book.

Bruce Janssen was the copy editor and worked his magic on the manuscript, turning it into the copy you see here.

Many thanks to Shannon Littlejohn, the proofreader, for taking her "grammar hammer" to the final manuscript.

I am thankful to the KLC family: board members, staff, faculty, coaches, alumni champions, community leadership program facilitators, university partners and business/private-sector partners. Together, we have created a special, game-changing organization. It is the utmost professional privilege to serve as president and CEO of this wonderful and dedicated family.

As usual, Clare McClaren of Novella Brandhouse applied her design magic and created yet another visually stunning KLC publication. Where would KLC be after all these years without her talent?

This project never would have happened without Carrie Lindeman serving as project manager. She organized the writers, kept tabs on the whole project and used her considerable skill to prod me to produce draft chapters. Her enthusiasm for the project and willingness to "raise the heat" was much appreciated.

Kristi Zukovich and Chase Willhite from the Kansas Health Foundation encouraged this project and were key strategic thought partners.

The data in the footnotes throughout the book come from the TCC Group, our evaluation partner. I am thankful to our friends at the TCC Group, especially Kate Locke who has been evaluating the KLC from the beginning. We've learned much from her efforts and our work is stronger today because of our partnership.

STEVE
COEN

MARTY
LINKSKY

RON
HEIFETZ

DAVID
CHRISLIP

BRUCE
JANSSEN

SHANNON
LITTLEJOHN

CLARE
MCCLAREN

CARRIE
LINDEMAN

KRISTI
ZUKOVICH

CHASE
WILLHITE

KATE
LOCKE

ACKNOWLEDGMENTS CONT.

Joanna, Kate, Jack and Lizzie O'Malley deserve the most thanks of all. My wife and children have been the most supportive family a president and CEO could ask for. Joanna's heart is in KLC, too. And the kids have grown up hearing about leadership and the common good. I am grateful for their patience with me as this project came to the finish line and for the love and support that has fueled and sustained me during these 10-plus years of the KLC.

JOANNA
O'MALLEY

KATE
O'MALLEY

JACK
O'MALLEY

LIZZIE
O'MALLEY

ABOUT THE AUTHOR

Ed O'Malley is the founding president and CEO of the Kansas Leadership Center. A former state legislator and gubernatorial aide, Ed started the center in 2007.

Ed is a proud graduate of Kansas State University and bleeds purple with his Wildcats in all sports. On summer evenings, Ed can often be found in a well-worn powder blue ball cap, cheering on his beloved Kansas City Royals.

On the personal side, Ed's an avid runner. He's participated in several marathons and a couple of what he refers to as "ill-advised" ultramarathons.

Ed is married to his childhood sweetheart, Joanna, whom he met on a school bus in the seventh grade. They are the parents of three children: Kate, Jack and Lizzie.

Stay up-to-date with Ed on Twitter @eomalley.

OTHER BOOKS BY ED O'MALLEY

"Your Leadership Edge: Lead Anytime, Anywhere"
by Ed O'Malley and Amanda Cebula

"For the Common Good: Redefining Civic Leadership"
by David Chrislip and Ed O'Malley

"For the Common Good Participant Handbook "
by Ed O'Malley, Julia Fabris McBride and Amy Nichols

WHAT'S
RIGHT
WITH
KANSAS